AGE OF CONTEXT

Mobile, Sensors, Data and the Future of Privacy

ROBERT SCOBLE & SHEL ISRAEL

Foreword by Marc Benioff

PATRICK BREWSTER PRESS
Age of Context: Mobile, Sensors, Data and the Future of Privacy
Robert Scoble and Shel Israel

Editor: Harry Miller
Cover Design: Nico Nicomedes
Interior Design: Shawn Welch

Published in the United States by Patrick Brewster Press
ISBN-13: 978-1-4923-4843-6
ISBN-10: 1-4923484-3-0

1st Edition
Printed by CreateSpace, a DBA of On-Demand Publishing, LLC

Also by Robert Scoble

Naked Conversations
The Conversational Corporation

Also by Shel Israel

Naked Conversations
The Conversational Corporation
Twitterville
Stellar Presentations

About the Authors

Robert Scoble is among the world's best-known tech journalists. In his day job as Startup Liaison for Rackspace, the Open Cloud Computing Company, Scoble travels the world looking for what's happening on technology's bleeding edge. He's interviewed thousands of executives and technology innovators and reports for Rackspace TV and in social media. He can be found at scobleizer.com. You can email him at Scobleizer@gmail.com, and on social networks as Robert Scoble.

Shel Israel helps businesses tell their stories in engaging ways as a writer, consultant and presentation coach. He writes *The Social Beat* column for Forbes and has contributed editorially to BusinessWeek, Dow Jones, Fast Company and American Express Open Forum. He has been a keynote speaker more than 50 times on five continents. You can follow him at http://blogs.forbes.com/shelisrael and talk to him at shelisrael1@gmail.com or on most social networks as shelisrael.

Thanks to Our Sponsors

T he book publishing business has become more daunting in recent times. In order to invest eight months of fulltime work on this project, we are grateful to the following companies who financed our effort.

Rackspace® Hosting (NYSE: RAX) is the open cloud company and founder of OpenStack®, the standard open-source operating system for cloud computing. Rackspace delivers its renowned Fanatical Support® to more than 200,000 business customers from data centers on four continents. Rackspace is a leading provider of hybrid clouds, which enable businesses to run their workloads where they run most effectively—whether on the public cloud, a private cloud, dedicated servers, or a combination of these platforms.

Visit www.rackspace.com.

EasilyDo gets you the right information and gets things done. It is the only mobile and wearable smart assistant that makes sure you never miss anything. EasilyDo works proactively and contextually to do things like check traffic before your commute, warn you of bad weather, organize contacts, track packages, celebrate birthdays, and more. With new Do Its (features) launched at a rapid pace, EasilyDo continues to lead the pack in innovation.

www.Easilydo.com

BetaWorks is a tightly linked network of ideas, people, capital, products and data united in imaginative ways to build out a more connected world. Our purpose is to build the most beneficial, most transformative products the socially connected world has ever seen. And we do everything we can to facilitate that goal. We also invest in other companies, because at the end of the day, investing makes us better builders.

http://betaworks.com/purpose

◣ AUTODESK.

Autodesk helps people imagine, design and create a better world. Everyone—from design professionals, engineers and architects to digital artists, students and hobbyists—uses Autodesk software to unlock their creativity and solve important challenges.

http://www.autodesk.com/

bing

Bing is the search engine from Microsoft. It was introduced in 2009 with a mission to empower people with knowledge — to answer any question and provide useful tools to help you best accomplish your goals, from the everyday to the extraordinary.

http://www.bing.com

charity: water

Charity:water We received an anonymous donation on behalf of this nonprofit organization on a mission to bring clean and safe drinking water to every person on the planet. They fund water solutions in developing countries around the world, restoring health and time to rural communities. charity: water uses 100% of public donations in the field, and proves each completed water project with photos and GPS coordinates on a map.

http://www.charitywater.org

Additional Contributors

Mindsmack is an award-winning digital agency.
http://www.mindsmack.com

Contents

Foreword

J ust a few months ago, I was headed out to a conference on the East Coast and tweeted from the plane (tweeted from the plane, mind you!), "Can't wait to get to Boston. Staying at the X hotel. Hope to have dinner at Rialto and see the Sox play tomorrow."

A few hours later, I walked into the hotel and was exuberantly greeted, "Welcome Mr. Benioff, we're so glad you are here. We saw your tweet. The restaurant you wanted to try? We have a table for you. And the tickets for tomorrow's game? They are on your nightstand, ready for you."

Wow. Amazing. Dream travel experience, right?

Yes, alas, it was just a dream. That is not what happened in the Boston hotel. Not at all. Instead, I checked in and they said, "Here are your keys."

But, it could have happened. And, it should have happened. (I can't even name the hotel because it's so embarrassing that they did not do this. But how phenomenal of a story would it have been if they did?)

Technology has unlocked incredible new ways for companies to connect with customers. The fact is, we have more data and more insight about the customer than ever before, and customers expect companies to use it. Now, companies cannot proceed with business as usual. They need to change and advance to meet the rising expectations of modern customers.

Today, we are in the midst of a customer revolution where the world is being reshaped by the convergence of social and mobile cloud technologies. The combination of these technologies enables us to connect everything together in a new way and is dramatically transforming the way we live and work.

Now, cloud computing over powerful LTE wireless networks is delivering on the promise of billions of computers interconnecting. Not just the mobile phones in our pockets, but different kinds of computers—our watches, our cameras, our cars, our refrigerators, our toothbrushes. Every aspect of our lives is somehow on the network, a wireless network, and in the cloud. This is the third wave of computing.

Research firm IDC reports that there will be 3.5 billion networked products by 2015. Compare that to 1.7 billion networked PCs and it's clear that the "Internet of Things" has arrived. With it, and with everything connected to the network, we enter an amazing new world of possibilities.

The big change here is that technology is becoming intuitive. It is starting to understand where you are and where you are likely to be going, and it can help you on your way. Connected technologies make your customers happier and accordingly, your revenues bigger.

In the connected world, customers are no longer just a number or account; they are unique human beings with a distinct set of needs. They have a powerful voice that they know how to use. They want a relationship on equal terms, and they expect to be at the center of your world. Companies must listen and engage and earn their trust every day.

That's why innovative companies are connecting employees, partners and products in new ways to align around customers like never before. I see our customers transforming into customer companies by building connected products that can communicate status updates, reports and other information in real time. Philips, a visionary consumer-centric company, is using technology to deliver innovations that matter to its customers. It uses our software to connect millions of products—from toothbrushes and coffee-makers, to new LED lighting products—onto a single customer network. (I'm looking forward to the connected next gen toothbrush that will send a report to my dentist.)

Toyota is using our software to connect dealers, customers, cars and devices. It is already building connections with customers into the more than 8 million cars it manufactures each year. Cars now have the capability to tweet status updates to their drivers. They can anticipate your actions so they can provide the service information that you need. Shigeki Tomoyama, managing officer at Toyota, calls it "a new kind of car, almost like an iPhone on wheels."

GE is another leading example. GE Aviation is building closer connections to its customers—and making its products more socially connected. The new GEnx jet engine—currently flying on Boeing's new 787 Dreamliner—can provide newsfeeds that can be accessed by service teams on their mobile devices to ultimately help reduce maintenance costs and increase engine lifespan.

The big question is how we will adapt to keep up with these changes. The *Age of Context* helps show us the way. The book examines five technology forces: mobile, social media, big data, sensors, and location-based technologies. It reports on sensors being installed everywhere from neighboring planets to traffic signals, and even in our workout shoes and toasters. It demonstrates how to leverage Big Data, and high-speed, high-scale cloud databases that allow near-instant analysis of terabytes of data. It reveals the next-generation mobile apps, which are customized and can anticipate what you want and need. It examines mature social media, highly personalized networks that will understand what you want in the context of where you are and what you are doing. It shows advances in wearable computers that not only add a hands-free ability, but that can become our assistants or coaches.

Technology always moves ahead—and this is the next evolution. And, like any evolution, adapting is what enables us to survive and thrive in an always-changing world. This book, which is written with inspiration and hope, shows how this new age will be good for us and for our health, for the education of our kids and for our businesses. It shows us how it will make our lives better.

Be prepared to see the future in these pages: glass in homes and skyscrapers that adjusts to mood and weather conditions and lets airplane pilots see through fog—all because the "glass understands the context of its environment." You'll read about mobile apps that know your calendar and what's at the dry cleaners so it can help you pick what to wear. In the not-so-distant future, we will have prosthetic devices sensitive to touch connected to human nerves and operating from brain commands. There will be exoskeletons that empower paraplegics to walk without assistance. It is truly a brave new world.

I have been in the tech industry for 35 years and what I love about it the most is that the only constant is change. We are now in the most transformative time of our industry. Veteran tech journalists Robert Scoble and Shel Israel walk us through these changes with compelling stories and insightful explanations. They have written an important book with the *Age of Context*. They see what's coming and reveal a very exciting picture of the future—and get us ready, which is critical because it's already here.

Marc Benioff

Founder, Chairman and CEO of salesforce.com

Introduction:
Storm's Coming

Computing is not about computers any more. It is about living.

Nicholas Negroponte, co-founder MIT Media Labs[†††]

A storm of change is coming.

In the 2005 movie *Batman Begins,* the caped guy appears out of nowhere to deliver a cryptic message to Commissioner Gordon about the short-term future of Gotham City. "Storm's coming," he warns and, just as suddenly as he appears, he is gone.

For the next two hours of the movie all hell breaks loose. Finally, peace is restored. When people resume their normal lives after so much tumult and trouble, they discover life after the storm is better than it was before.

[†††] This text contains multiple references that can be found in the links section starting on page 179. Throughout the text, sections that contain hyperlink references will be marked with the triple-dagger symbol (†††).

Change is inevitable, and the disruption it causes often brings both inconvenience and opportunity. The recent history of technology certainly proves that. In the pages that follow, we describe contextual computing, the latest development in the evolution of technological change, and discuss how it will affect nearly all aspects of your life and work.

We are not caped crusaders, but we are here to prepare you for an imminent storm. Tumult and disruption will be followed by improvements in health, safety, convenience and efficiency.

Who Are These Guys?

We are two veteran Silicon Valley journalists, covering two interdependent communities: technology and business. We've been hanging out in tech circles for most of our professional lives and have spent many, many hours interviewing tech newsmakers.

Robert Scoble has become one of the world's best-known and most respected reporters of tech innovation. Shel Israel has provided reports and analysis for private business and as a freelancer for *BusinessWeek, Fast Company,* Dow Jones Publishing and currently *Forbes.com.*

A quick aside about voice: We occasionally discuss each other in the third person. It's the simplest way we know to maintain clarity when two of us are writing.

This is our fourth collaboration. Our biggest previous success was a book called *Naked Conversations: How Blogs are Changing the Way Businesses Talk with Customers,*[†††] which came out in the first week of 2006. *Naked Conversations* concluded by declaring that what we now call social media was bringing the world into a new age, one we called the Age of Conversation, a term that has endured so far.

As common as the topic of context has become in Scoble's technology-centric world, Israel has heard very little mention of it in business circles. Most businesspeople are still trying to push rocks uphill toward business recovery.

However, history indicates that when the tech community is unified, focused and excited about a topic, as it is about context, it almost always follows that they will make waves that land on the shores of commerce. Although this book introduces some thought leaders, the business community overall is not thinking much about context right now. But they will soon be productizing it and using it for competitive advantage.

Context Through Google Glass

Google Glass is the product that is raising public awareness, excitement and concerns about contextual computing. This wearable device is discussed in depth in Chapter 2. It is like nothing that has previously existed, containing sensors, a camera, a microphone, and a prism for projecting information in front of your eyes. It has more computing power than the 1976 Cray-1 super-computer that cost $8.8 million.[†††] It weighs a mere 49 grams and serves as a highly personalized assistant that accompanies you through your daily life.

A simple example is how Glass displays your specific flight information as you walk into the airline terminal. It can do that because the system knows your location and your calendar and can sense where you're looking. The more it knows about you and your activity patterns, the better it can serve your current needs—and even predict what you might want next.

Thad Starner, a technical lead/manager on Google's Glass team and associate professor of computing at Georgia Tech, is a trailblazer in wearable contextual technology. As he explains on his Google+ page,[†††] "For over 20 years I have worn a computer in my everyday life as an intelligent assistant, the longest such experience known." He also coined the term "augmented reality" to describe the assistive experience.

In 1991, Starner's doctoral thesis[†††] mentioned "that on-body systems can sense the user's context ...." A little more than 20 years later, the necessary technologies have caught up with his prediction.

As we started investigating contextual technologies we quickly saw implications going far beyond this well-publicized digital eyewear. In 2012, we watched all sorts of wearable technologies migrate from R&D labs into a wide variety of products and services. We found a great many promising entrepreneurs who were selling or planning innovative products for retail, transportation, government, medicine and home use that were all built on the premise of serving users better by knowing more about them and their environments.

Contextual Building Blocks

In *The Perfect Storm*,[†††] author Sebastian Junger described a rare but fierce weather phenomenon caused by the convergence of three meteorological forces: warm air, cool air, and tropical moisture. Such natural occurrences cause 100-foot waves, 100-mph winds and—at least until recently—occur about once every 50 to 100 years.

Our perfect storm is composed not of three forces, but five, and they are technological rather than meteorological: mobile devices, social media, big data, sensors and location-based services. You'll learn more about them in Chapter 1 and how they're already causing disruption and making waves. As discrete entities, each force is already part of your life. Together, they have created the conditions for an unstoppable perfect storm of epic proportion: the Age of Context.

Those forces are made possible by the maturation of some enabling technologies. Up to this point, computers either filled a room or sat on a table. Today, miniaturization resulting from silicon engineering has enabled the power of a supercomputer to fit in a wearable or mobile device. Previously, computers didn't know anything about you or your context—not where you were, whom you were with or what you were doing. Today, the Age of Context brings a new kind of mobile or wearable computer that can wirelessly interact with dozens, if not hundreds, of sensors on or around you. This device also has access to all of humankind's collected knowledge.

Through the use of many different types of sensors, our mobile devices now emulate three of our five senses. Camera sensors give them eyes, and microphone sensors serve as ears; capacitive sensors enable them to feel our touch on their screens. They can't yet detect fragrance—but our guess is that such a capability is coming soon.

The so-called Internet of Things enables many common appliances, fixtures and devices to communicate with systems due to the availability of radical new low-cost and miniaturized sensors. Microsoft Kinect for Xbox, for example, has a 3D sensor that can see your heartbeat just by looking at your skin.

When we talk about "the system knowing about you," that knowledge depends on machine learning and database computation breakthroughs that couldn't be imagined when Microsoft researcher Jim Gray[†††] turned on Microsoft's first terabyte database back in December 1997. Similarly, significant innovations and accuracy improvements in voice recognition make systems like Apple's Siri, Google Now and Google Voice Search possible.

The foundation for the Age of Context—all of these technologies working together—is the cloud computing infrastructure, which continues to grow exponentially in capability and capacity. And it had better keep growing: A self-driving car, which we describe in Chapter 5, generates about 700 megabytes of data per second. We talked with GM, Ford, Toyota—and Google—about what would happen if every car had that technology. Well, for one thing, today's cloud computing technology would melt down.

Rackspace, a cloud hosting provider and Scoble's employer, was the first and largest sponsor of this book. Since 2009, it has funded Scoble to travel the world interviewing hundreds of entrepreneurs and innovators. One reason for such support is that it had also seen an increase in resource-intensive services and data flows.

By coincidence, Rackspace also provides the infrastructure for many of the companies we discuss in this book. Years before we teamed up for this book, Rackspace was exploring potentially world-changing or disruptive trends. In response to those trends, it built a new hybrid cloud to enable companies to scale and address new privacy concerns it realized the new contextual technologies would bring.

Rackspace asked Scoble, its public-facing point person, to independently dig into this new pattern and figure out what was going on. Thus began the 18-month journey that culminated in the publication of this book. So we appreciate Rackspace for its support and its insights.

The Tradeoff

Some of the technology you'll read about can be a bit discomforting: Cars without drivers. Calendars that send messages on your behalf. Front doors that unlock and open when they see you approach. But those issues are fairly straightforward; people will either embrace the new technology or they won't.

The larger looming issue is the very real loss of personal privacy and the lack of transparency about how it happens. The marvels of the contextual age are based on a tradeoff: the more the technology knows about you, the more benefits you will receive. That can leave you with the chilling sensation that big data is watching you. In the vast majority of cases, we believe the coming benefits are worth that tradeoff. Whether or not you come to the same conclusion, we all will need to understand the multiple issues that will be impacting the future of privacy.

Weather the Storm

All indications are that the changes ushered in by the Age of Context will be more significant and fundamental than what has occurred in the previous era, and they are likely to occur faster. We hope you can use this book as a framework to understand the contextual developments that will take place over the next few years. We hope you take it in context and that it will help you adjust to the changes in your work and your life.

We also hope you will find the book fun to read. We tell you many stories about amazing people and uncanny technology. We hope to convince you that embracing contextual technology is very much in your interest. Above all, we hope to prepare you so you can survive and thrive through the coming titanic storm.

CHAPTER 1

The Five Forces

The force is an energy field created by all living things. It surrounds us and penetrates us. It binds the galaxy together.

Obi-Wan Kenobi, *Star Wars*

They're everywhere. The five forces of context are at your fingertips when you touch a screen. They know where you are and in what direction you are headed when you carry a smartphone. They are in your car to warn you when you are too close to something else. They are in traffic lights, stores and even pills.

The five forces are changing your experience as a shopper, a customer, a patient, a viewer or an online traveler. They are also changing businesses of all sizes.

All five of these forces—mobile, social media, data, sensors and location—are enjoying an economic sweet spot. They are in a virtuous cycle. Rapid adoption is driving prices down, which in turn drives more adoption, which completes the cycle by driving prices down further.

This means these five forces are in the hands of more people every day, and it means almost every business will have to adjust course to include context in their strategies, just as they had to do at the advent of other forces of dramatic change, like personal computing or the web.

Forward-thinking business leaders and tech evangelists are already using these forces to prosper, while simultaneously making their customers and followers happier, and technologists are coming up with new contextual tools, toys and services at a breathtaking speed.

We told you a little bit about each of these five forces in our introduction and you are already familiar with most or all of them, but let's drill a little deeper to help you understand why each is so powerful.

Mobile

Sometime in 2012, the number of cellphones on Earth surpassed the number of people.[†††] By the end of the year, we had 120 million tablet computers and Gartner Group, a market analyst, predicted the number would grow to 665 million by 2016.[†††]

Whether or not these forecasts come close doesn't really matter. The point is there are going to be a whole lot of mobile devices around and, by simple arithmetic, most people in the developed world will be carrying around more than one of them at any given time.

Mobile is taking new forms. You've already heard much about Google Glass,[†††] but a lot more is going on in wearables than the new digital eyewear. Despite how new and different these products may seem, people are adopting them faster than many prognosticators anticipated.

Tech analyst Juniper Research[†††] estimates wearable computing will generate $800 million in revenue in 2013, rising to $1.5 billion in 2014. Annual unit sales of wearables will rise from 15 million in 2013 to 70 million by 2017. Personally, we think those numbers are very low, but we shall see.

Wearables are already in use for recreation, personal and business productivity, meeting new people, improving safety, fitness and health. We think wearables will be used in a great many more ways, some of which are yet to be imagined.

The mobile device often overlooked these days is the laptop. Laptops gave people an appreciation, even a hunger, for mobility. They untethered us from the desktop, but they really aren't contextual machines. They don't have sensors and they don't have operating systems that can run the mobile apps essential to context. These days, laptops feel heavy and awkward compared with other mobile options. In fact, laptops have become the new desktops. Most are left at home or in the office as we move around with more agile and contextual tools.

And costs are coming down, primarily because there's lots of competition. Even the barriers presented by expensive data plans are eroding because of challenges from upstart companies like Macheen[†††] and ItsOn,[†††] and most recently industry giants T-Mobile[†††] and Sprint.[†††]

The smartphone is now the primary device for most people—the one they live on and use most of the time. This has been made possible, of course, by the great migration of data from our individual computers into the cloud and it is now being strengthened by its accommodation of contextual applications.

We believe, despite innovations in next-generation laptops as well as the incredible hands-free capabilities of wearables, that for at least the next five to ten years the smartphone will be the wireless device of choice for most of the world's users.

We also believe that in both phones and tablets, the brand and the operating systems consumers choose are starting to matter less. The hardware forms from multiple suppliers are beginning to resemble each other and the devices perform extremely similar functions. This may be bad for the makers, but it is good for us users.

People will use such devices more as they become low-cost commodities. This means the streams of data being uploaded, and the amount of content being consumed by these devices, will increase exponentially.

The real mobile news is not in the devices themselves, but in how software has changed. A little over a decade ago, software was primarily loaded onto our desktop computers by inserting discs. Price-per-user was often well over $100 and occasionally exceeded $1000.

Today's software is small, inexpensive or free. It takes about 30 seconds to start using a mobile app. The average user downloads scores of them.

The *New York Times* estimated that the 100,000-plus worldwide mobile app publishers offered more than 1.2 million mobile apps by the end of 2011. According to Gartner,[†††] apps were downloaded over 45 billion times by the end of 2012—more than six apps for every man, woman and child on Earth and that number is continuously growing.

Mobile is the aggregator of our other four forces. It's where they all converge. Your device is your key to all the power of the internet. It is where the superstorm of context thunders into your life.

Social Media

In 2005, when we were researching *Naked Conversations,*[†††] fewer than 4 million people were using blogs, wikis and podcasts. The terms "social media" and "social networks" did not yet exist. Facebook had started, but at the time we dismissed it as an irrelevant niche service for Ivy League frat boys seeking dates. Twitter hadn't even been born.

Fast-forward to the beginning of 2013, when a billion tweets[†††] were posted every 48 to 72 hours and growth was exponential. Today, nearly 1.5 billion[†††] people are on social networks. Almost no successful modern business deploys a go-forward strategy that does not include social media. Almost every mobile app we mention in this book contains a social media component.

When organizations use social media wisely, companies and customers come closer together. Employees and users often collaborate on making products and services better.

Although most of us don't yet feel all warm and fuzzy about the modern enterprise, social media has empowered some of these gargantuan entities to present a more human face. We've come to recognize that behind the corporate curtain that displays a brand logo, real people are very often trying to serve customers better.

Smart companies have come to understand that social media enables them to cut costs and improve marketing, research, product development, recruiting, communications and support.

However, social media can also be abused and misused. Instead of using it to engage customers and prospects, some companies use it to shovel out marketing messages. This may seem effective in the short term, but in the long run it is usually a mistake. Social media is a two-way channel, and if you just send messages out, it's like using a phone only to talk, not listen.

What has changed in the seven years since we proclaimed its arrival in *Naked Conversations* is that social media is no longer a disruptive force. Instead it is a vital business component. Rather than being resisted, social media is now being woven into the very fabric of business.

Social media is essential to the new Age of Context. It is in our online conversations that we make it clear what we like, where we are and what we are looking for. As social media integrates with mobile, data, sensors, and location-based technologies, it serves as a fount of highly personalized content, and that content allows technology to understand the context of who you are, what you are doing and what you are likely to do next.

Data

We hear a great deal about data these days. A lot of it is about danger and size. Ironically, just about everything we enjoy and need online comes to us from data. It is the oxygen of the Age of Context. It is everywhere and it is essential.

Data is often referred to as "big data" because the amount that has been accumulated is so vast. Describing it in quantifiable terms is like trying to measure the universe or calculate how many angels can dance on a Pinterest pinhead.

Data is how we measure the internet. Back in 2005 Eric Schmidt,[†††] then CEO of Google, estimated the size of the internet[†††] at roughly 5 million terabytes. Today that's small potatoes. Every day, we expand the internet by half the size it was in 2005[†††]—and it continues to expand at an exponential rate.

IBM estimates[†††] that 90 percent of the world's data was created in the last two years. As co-authors Rick Smolan[†††] and Jennifer Erwitt stated in their exquisite photo book, *The Human Face of Big Data,*[†††] "Now, in the first day of a baby's life today, the world creates 70 times the data contained in the entire Library of Congress."

This means that every day of your life, more data is being uploaded than was created throughout all recorded history until just a couple of years ago.

So, there's lots of focus on the "big" aspect of data. It sometimes gives us the image of truckloads of data being heaped upon existing truckloads somewhere up in the cloud, creating a virtual mountain so immense it makes Everest look like a molehill.

In our opinion, the focus is on the wrong element: It's not the big data mountain that matters so much to people, it's those tiny little spoonfuls we extract whenever we search, chat, view, listen, buy—or do anything else online. The hugeness can intimidate, but the little pieces make us smarter and enable us to keep up with, and make sense of, an accelerating world.

We call this the miracle of little data.

In a couple of seconds, and on a single try, we find precisely the three tweets we are searching for. They are extracted from billions that we don't want and don't receive. Instagram can display exactly where you were on the planet when you clicked that cute shot of your puppy and not show you all the other places where other puppies were photographed.

You don't need to be a technologist to understand there is something amazing in our ability to find precisely the data we want—and only the data we want—in a song, email or restaurant review. It's like finding a diamond in a coalmine—every time we search—without dirtying ourselves in the coal.

We accomplish this because computers have developed the ability to recognize patterns in data streams and extract data based on who's asking for it. It is a complicated process that happens usually in less than two seconds and most of us don't fully understand how it works. The miracle is that you can enjoy the results and even take them for granted. All you need to know is how to work a few simple apps on your mobile phone.

Until recently, only the wealthiest and most powerful organizations could extract data effectively from databases. First, a computer professional who could speak the language of a database software program had to put the data into a structure that the machine could understand, and then know how to retrieve it later. It was hard, and those of us who had to use such structured databases found them cumbersome and slow to produce results that mattered.

Most of us are a much messier lot when it comes to data. We generally prefer Post-It notes to some arcane language called SQL or DB2. We have created a messy internet filled with text, sites and posts that do not adhere to database language structures and, therefore, can not be found in structured databases.

When data started coming at a daily rate of 70 times the contents of the Library of Congress, programmers simply could not keep structuring and entering it anywhere near the speed at which people produced it. So next-generation companies like Google started building networks of gigantic data centers that employed millions of computers to host all the data being produced.

Storing this data was the smaller of two challenges. The bigger one was figuring out how everyday people could extract the little spoonfuls they wanted from inside the new unstructured big data mountains.

Google again led the way. Until 2012, the essence of its data search engine was Page Rank,††† which used complex mathematical equations, or algorithms, to understand connections between web pages and then rank them by relevance in search results.

Before Google, we got back haystacks when we searched for needles. Then we had to sift through pages and pages of possible answers to find the one right for us. Page Rank started to understand the rudimentary context of a search. It could tell by your inquiry pattern that when you searched for "park in San Francisco" you wanted greenery and not some place to leave your car.

Essentially, Google reversed the data equation. Instead of you learning to speak in a machine language, Google started to make machines recognize your natural language. This has made all the difference in the world.

When Facebook rapidly evolved into the world's biggest site, it made a series of forward leaps related to searching. First, it came up with the social graph,††† which examines relationships between people instead of data. It extrapolated relevant data by examining graphical representations rather than strings of text.

Next, Facebook created a Graph API (Application Programming Interface) that enabled third-party developers to connect and share data with the Facebook platform using common verbs such as "read," "listen to," "like," "comment on" and so forth.

More recently—and significantly—Facebook introduced Graph Search,[†††] which might well evolve into the first significant challenge to Google's search engine dominance. Instead of using keyword searches to find pages such as "Boston + lobster restaurants," Graph Search allows users to use natural language to ask questions such as, "Restaurants nearby that my friends like." Then, instead of having a spider crawl pages of data on the web, it finds relevant content in conversations your friends have had.

Graph Search provides faster, easier and more contextually relevant results because the Facebook technology is able to extract most of what you hope to find. Google uses links to decide relevancy; Facebook uses your friends and an understanding of your social behavior.

That's a sizeable shift, and one that will be important as we head into the Age of Context. And Facebook isn't alone. In our research on data, we found dozens of new companies using new methods to extract unstructured data. All were open source companies whose founders seem more intent on empowering the masses than they are in helping big companies aggregate dirt on their customers or push ads into their faces. Many are using graphs instead of tables to get better results outside the walls of the Facebook garden.

One such company is Neo Technology[†††] of San Mateo, California. Founder Emil Eifrem explained to us the importance of graphical versus text-based searches as a modern confirmation of the old adage that a picture is worth a thousand words.[†††]

Database technology is evolving beyond graphs. A company called ai-one, inc.,[†††] is making progress on "biologically inspired intelligent agents" that will deliver results by searching for ideas,[†††] instead of merely keywords. In short, their technology builds tools that emulate the way the human brain works. Essentially, humans recognize patterns—sometimes highly complex ones. We can detect the fundamental features and meaning of text, time and visual data, key components of context.

Pattern recognition, which started just a few years ago, is now reaching the state where database search tools are starting to *think* like people think. They don't yet do it as effectively as we humans do it, but they do it faster and far more efficiently.

There is a dark side to these growing capabilities. We should watch for the unintended consequences that always seem to accompany significant change. The potential for data abuse and the loss of privacy head the list of concerns. Eli Pariser wrote a passionate and sincere argument about the loss of privacy in his 2011 book, *The Filter Bubble.*[†††]

Pariser took a dark view of the fact that virtually every online site collects, shares and sells user data. He talked about how large organizations use data to stereotype people and then assume they know what we want to see and hear. By getting our eyeballs to stick to their web pages they then get us to click on ads they target at us.

The book gave the impression that through data, big organizations are watching us in a very Orwellian way. It raised concerns about identity theft and loss of privacy and created a fear that big companies will control what we see. Pariser scared the hell out of a lot of people who were already unsettled about this topic.

He served as the prosecutor making the case against big data, and he made a good case. In fact, there is truth to what he had to say and people should consider Pariser's perspective as they make their own decisions about what to do and not do in the Age of Context.

In our view, though, Pariser presented a one-sided perspective on a multi-sided and highly granular issue. *The Filter Bubble* overlooked the world-improving changes that big data is making.

As Neo's Eifrem sees it, "Fundamentally, companies like Neo build hammers. You can use them to build or to smash. Yes, there will be abuses and we must be vigilant about that, but the best solution to empowering people to find and learn what they need is contained in the new databases. Big data allows everyone to easily get better results for what they are looking for through personalization of search results."

We share Eifrem's perspective. If Pariser is the prosecutor, then perhaps you should regard us as big data's defense team. Sometimes, abusers will do horrible things with data they stole, bought or otherwise obtained. But, percentagewise, most data helps you and most companies use it in reputable ways, usually to serve customers better.

Unquestionably, the genie has long since left the bottle. As Pariser points out, nearly every site collects data. If you use the internet at all, data is being collected on you. Some people may choose to opt out of the internet for this reason, but if you do that, you are opting out of modern times.

Or, you can limit your depth of involvement. Many people use Facebook just to talk with people they already know and perhaps find a few long-lost friends, sharing comments with a handful of acquaintances. Shel Israel's wife Paula is among them. She is quite happy with her limited use of the platform. Despite her recognition of the imminent Age of Context, she values her privacy enough to opt out of a number of social media options.

Conversely, Robert Scoble spends many of his waking hours on Facebook. He shares nearly everything about his life online. He is so transparent that he sometimes makes Israel nervous. But his Facebook presence has made him among the world's best-known technology innovators and that has very favorably impacted his professional life.

More than a million people follow Scoble on his social networks. Some become news sources for his Rackspace video work.[†††] He gets invited to events all over the world. Scoble believes that the more he tells Facebook and other online sites, the more valuable his online experience will be.

Shel Israel, and most people, fall somewhere in between Scoble and Paula Israel. Perhaps you should have the right to opt in before companies start taking and sharing our data but, like Paula Israel, you do have the ability to opt out. When you do, sites will know less about you and you need to expect you will get less from them. Over time there is the very real possibility you will be left behind.

Sensors

Sensors are simple little things that measure and report on change, and in so doing they emulate the five human senses. They are being attached to all sorts of living and inert objects so they can share what they observe. Because sensors seem to be watching and listening to you, as well as understanding what you are doing, they, like big data, sometimes freak people out.

Sensors go back a very long way. In the mid-1600s Evangelista Torricelli, an Italian physicist, invented a way to measure atmospheric pressure by using mercury in a vacuum tube called a Torricellian Tube. Most people know it as a barometer.

Sensors' full capability began about 50 years ago when factory automation started to come into play. Unlike people, sensors work tirelessly, never needing sleep and never demanding a raise. They notice changes where humans miss them, thus ensuring labels are correctly affixed to bottles moving through a factory assembly line. They are used in nuclear power plants for early detection of leaks.

Some semiconductor foundries, such as TSMC in Taiwan, are attempting to build what's known as "lights-out factories," where sensors will eliminate the need for any employees at all. Unconfirmed reports indicate they are coming close.

By the early 1990s, sensors had become so inexpensive and so collectively powerful when used in networks that engineers were starting to believe the number of ways and places they could be useful was almost limitless.

By 2001, the conversation started to expand into what could happen when sensors were used to communicate over the web. Kevin Ashton,[†††] an MIT technology pioneer, developed the concept of inanimate objects talking with people—and with each other—over the internet in global mesh networks. He called this the Internet of Things,[†††] and that vision is now reality. Half of the conversations on the internet involve sensor-enabled machines that, more often than not, talk with other machines.

Sensors exist everywhere on Earth, as well as above and below it. Instead of killing canaries in mines, we now use sensors to detect problems and alert people. They enable the Mars rover *Curiosity* to search for water and life and report what they find to people on Earth. Jet engines on commercial planes talk in a social network with technicians to increase fuel economy.

Sensors keep health officials informed if you are epileptic, have heart problems or suffer from vertigo. The FDA has approved a digestible sensor embedded in a pill. After you swallow, the sensor reports data to technicians; hopefully soon sensors will eliminate many invasive tests. Sensors are being used in robots to make them behave in ways that are incredibly humanlike.

The watershed moment when sensors became a contextual force took place in January 2007 when Steve Jobs introduced the iPhone. This was the first successful mobile device to sport a touch screen—made possible through a tiny sensor in the glass. The phone included other sensors that let you flip from horizontal to vertical view, find Wifi and connect to a Bluetooth listening device. An accelerometer sensor even enabled the phone to protect itself if you dropped it.

Today, smartphones contain an average of seven sensors. A rapidly growing number of mobile apps use them to know where you are and what you are doing. Such sensor surveillance may sound creepy to some, but it enables mobile devices to provide users with highly personalized benefits, from a special offer on an item in a store window to a warning of a road hazard around the next curve. Sensors know when you are heading or leaving home and can adjust your contextual thermostat accordingly.

Phones know where you are and where you have been. Police are now getting subpoenas to establish or refute alibis of suspects through their phone's location records. Police investigators use them to reconstruct the last hours in a murder victim's life and—like it or not—your phones are keeping an ongoing log of what happens wherever you take them. They already know what building you are in. Not too far into the future, your mobile device will also know what floor you are on, what room you are in, and in which direction you are moving.

Sensors are being used in a number of promising mobile applications that alert stores when loyal customers walk in. They warn you when your car wanders out of its lane. They know when you are touching a box on a retail shelf, or when your running shoes need replacing.

For example, if you use a mobile app called Highlight,[†††] you'll be able to find people who interest you and who are physically within a football field's distance from where you stand. Likewise, when you walk through the door, stores will know whether you are a frequent buyer or someone with an arrest record for shoplifting, and you will be treated in the context of who you are.

Sensors can tell you where your keys are[†††] or who your dog likes.[†††] They are embedded in prosthetic hands,[†††] restoring the sensation of touch. In an upcoming chapter on the contextual city we'll explain how sensors can see changes in traffic patterns and adjust signal lights in response, and how sensors can warn first responders of unseen hazards and show them where injured or unconscious people can be found amid smoke and rubble.

We'll tell you about how they have alerted people to grave danger. In Japan in 2011 sensors warned officials 65 seconds before the Tohoku earthquake and tsunami[†††] hit, giving them just enough time to stop bullet trains heading toward peril, thus saving thousands of lives. Following the disaster, sensors helped citizens build a high-radiation heat map that warned them of places to avoid.

In fact, sensors will play a role in nearly every chapter of this book. The same sensors you already use in today's mobile devices can tell your car when to hit the brakes and avoid collision if you are too slow to respond. They know whether you are sky diving or sleeping. In homes, they know if there is too much smoke or if the lights should be turned on.

One mobile app we like is Shark Net,[†††] which uses sensors attached to buoys and robotic surfboards toting underwater cameras to track shark movements. Over time, marine biologists are starting to understand the patterns of each individual shark and are getting good at predicting when a specific shark can be expected to appear in a particular place. Shark Net was designed to serve marine biologists, but you can bet surfers are using it as well.

The military uses sensors on vehicles and body armor[†††] to detect environmental changes and head trauma. Sensors can detect motion caused by enemy combatants and their bullets. Some veterinarians use motion sensors to detect lameness in racehorses.[†††]

An environmentally friendly company, Sensible Self, makes GreenGoose, cute little wireless stickers containing motion sensors that allow you to track anything that moves, from a pet or child to your phone, or even to check if your spouse left the toilet seat up.[†††]

Melanie Martella, Executive Editor of *Sensors* magazine,††† introduced us to the concept of sensor fusion,††† a fast-emerging technology that takes data from disparate sources to come up with more accurate, complete and dependable data. Sensor fusion enables the same sense of depth that is available in 3D modeling, which is used for all modern design and construction, as well as the magic of special effects in movies.

Sensors will understand if you are pilfering office supplies or engaging in a clandestine office affair. If you are a burglar, your phone might end up bearing witness against you and, in fact, your car will be able to testify if you were parked in an area you deny having visited—and it will be able to report when you were there, and if it was you in the car.

Many of these scenarios are already part of your life. Soon they will become even more integral and they will be inextricable from life itself in the Age of Context.

Location

In September 2012, Apple launched its own mobile maps. It took very little time for the public to realize that they were so awful as to be comedic. But the humor got lost if you were using them to find your way along a snowy road late at night.

Apple Maps somehow managed to erase famous landmarks from their sites in the world's major cities; others were relocated under bodies of water. Drivers reported that turn-by-turn voice directions were misguiding them, occasionally urging them to take abrupt turns mid-span on suspension bridges.

The maps were so flawed that CEO Tim Cook soon publicly apologized, encouraging customers to use competing products, including Google Maps. It was a head-scratcher. How could a company, universally acclaimed for unmatched product elegance, make such an unmitigated gaffe?

Some pointed to a bitter and public divorce between Apple and Google. Steve Jobs had considered Google Android to be a direct rip-off of Apple's iOS operating system. Could Apple Maps have simply been a crudely devised and poorly executed act of revenge against a powerful former ally? We think not. In our view, Apple made a huge mistake, but it was strategically motivated and not part of a petty Silicon Valley vendetta.

Although Google and Apple historically had lots of good reasons to be allies, they were destined to become the rivals they now are. In the past, tech companies were pretty much divided between hardware and software, so an alliance between world leaders in each of the two categories was formidable, to say the least.

Apple was clearly the pacesetter in world-changing mobile hardware. But hardware eventually becomes a commodity. These days many of Apple's competitors offer similar and occasionally superior features, often at lower prices.

When search ruled the universe, Google was perched on the throne. However, Google saw they would need to achieve more to retain their position and became adept and strategic as an online software provider.

Business models for Apple and Google have been rapidly evolving in recent years, and Facebook is a new pretender to that throne. Google, Apple and Facebook now understand the biggest issue facing them today is being where people will spend the most time online. That is not a device issue but a mobile app issue.

To remain a leader, Apple and Google each needed to vie for online time, for alliances with third-party developers and to provide platforms that make those apps valuable. For Google that meant having its own operating system; for Apple it meant having maps because it saw the unquestionable value of location-based services. For Apple, and many companies, mobile apps are the secret sauce of the Age of Context; mobile mapping is the most strategic of all categories.

Caterina Fake,[†††] CEO and founder of Findery,[†††] a location-based platform, explains it best in a statement that is simultaneously obvious and profound: "Without location, there is no context." And for Apple, without context there will be no leadership.

So Apple and Google divorced. Today Android and iOS compete for mobile operating system dominance, and thus Apple had little choice but to develop its own maps. Its big mistake was not in the play, but in being unprepared for the enormous challenges they faced on an unrealistically short timeline and then blindly plowing forward.

By the time Apple Maps launched, Google had about 7000 employees working on its mobile maps. Matching that is nearly impossible for Apple, whose entire company has only 20,000 employees. Google has a seven-year lead in every aspect of the category. Now, Apple faces a formidable up ramp and they have amplified the problem by drawing attention to it and failing with their first shot. Apple Maps are improving in accuracy, but regaining user confidence and loyalty will take a long time.

We turned to Daniel Graf,[†††] Director of Google Mobile Maps, to explain just what it takes to build a map platform and to get some sense of where the company is going. Graf is not a professional cartographer. He's an entrepreneur with a background in consumer mobile software.

He's been at Google since 2011. Graf says that to do maps right, there are three essential components:

1. **Build a foundation**. The foundation of all maps is data. Google started by licensing data from other cartography companies. In 2007, it started gathering its own. By the time Graf talked with us in September 2012, the company had gathered geographically relevant data in 30 countries over seven years and had added such exotic places as the Galapagos Islands,[†††] where Darwin once explored. In most places, company employees drive around in specially equipped cars with "tons of sensors" that analyze everything from road width, direction street signs, localized spellings, etc. Then Google takes a look at the same streets and neighborhoods via satellite, which it makes available via Google Earth.

In the case of the Galapagos, Google sent in their Street View team, despite the fact that there are no streets on the pristine Pacific island. They reduced the technology contained in the usual cars to be small enough to fit in 40-pound backpacks so the team could carry them around the island. The project would not have been possible without tiny sensors, which also helped the team observe under water.

The Galapagos anecdote shows another reason that Graf seems unworried about a future Apple map project. You cannot win in maps by investing dollars; you have to invest time. "This is not a process that can be sped up," Graf says. It appears to us that Google's seven-year head start will be difficult to overtake.

2. **Keep Track of Changes**. Graf says that perhaps the most daunting challenge is keeping current with local data, which is in a state of constant flux. Street names, addresses and directions change all the time. A dry cleaner closes and a Starbucks opens at the same address. Old buildings get demolished and new ones rise. Google uses multiple sources to stay current, the most significant one being their users, who are encouraged to report mistakes when they find them.

3. **Personalize Through Integration.** Maps become more valuable when they have a sense of where people are, what they are doing and what they want to do next.

    Your software needs to understand the context when you type in 'Thai.' Do you want to find a south Asian country or a restaurant in Lower Manhattan? This is the area of greatest focus for Google Maps, and the need to understand personalization is spread across the company's growing collection of tightly integrated software, services and platforms. This integration lets each Google app share what it knows about you with other Google apps.

Graf noted that the first two components of success in mapping involve data, while the third involves context. He estimated it would take Apple about a year from the time we talked to catch up in the first two areas. He implied that by that point, Google would have leapfrogged ahead mostly by addressing the third issue.

We had the impression that Google's strategic goal is to become the ultimate contextual company, and we find them well positioned to become precisely that. It explains why Google is driving hard to produce Google Glass.

It explains still further why Google had to develop the Android operating system so it could evolve into the mobile platform that wins the who-knows-its-users-best contest. It also explains why Google+ does not aspire to become a head-to-head social network competitor with Facebook, but instead plans to be the social network most closely integrated with Google's expanding suite of contextual products.

Google wants to know you so well that it can predict what you will do next. It tries to answer your inquiries on any of its products based on the context of where you are. What time do Thai restaurants close in a specific neighborhood? Where's the cheapest parking? Is there a high crime rate in that area?

Will Apple ever catch up with Google? We have no idea, but we hope so. We don't root for one company over another. We remain steadfastly on the side of the user—and when we users have choices, innovation accelerates and prices drop.

A host of new location-based services from creative and brilliant startups have sprung up recently and we anticipate many more to come. They, of course, cannot work without maps—another reason Apple needs to get back into the game as fast as it can. These third-party apps cannot exist without maps because, as Caterina Fake says, without them there is no context.

The granddaddy of location-based services is Foursquare,[†††] which was founded way back in 2009. It is a location-based social network that lets users "check in" based on where they are. In its first two years, Foursquare attracted over 20 million registered users.[†††]

By 2013, Foursquare users had checked in more than a billion times, giving the company an astoundingly large database on shopper location and individual store preferences. For example, if you've shopped once a month for the last two years on Saturday mornings at the Costco in Everett, Massachusetts, Foursquare knows this. It can help nearby retailers offer you specials relevant to your purchasing habits, where you are likely to be at that time and day and whether you live or shop a few miles north of Boston.

If you also frequent Home Depot, Foursquare knows you might want to attend the Massachusetts Home Show[†††] in the city's Hynes Civic Auditorium. When you check in on Foursquare, show exhibitors may offer you special deals.

Foursquare remains popular, but a plethora of more sophisticated location-based mobile services have recently come to market. Some allow you to do all sorts of things based on your personal preferences. When you are snow skiing they will know where you are located, how fast you are going and thus when you will arrive at the lodge, and when to have that Irish coffee they know you favor ready to be poured as you amble up to the bar.

Perhaps you paid for your adult beverage in advance with a web-stored credit card activated by a nod, blink or gesture your digital eyewear understood. Some software doesn't know you at all but sends offers to a map location, so anyone who checks on their map gets the offer when they are nearby.

This and many other nascent revolutionary applications of contextual software are right around the corner.

From a contextual perspective, we hold Google in particularly high regard, but the real game-changing development is the gadget Scoble is wearing on our back cover—Google Glass.

CHAPTER 2
Through the Glass, Looking

Right now, most of us look at the people with Google Glass like the dudes who first walked around with the big brick phones.

Amber Naslund, SideraWorks[†††]

The first of them went to Sergey Brin, Larry Page, and Eric Schmidt. Brin, who runs Project Glass, the company's much-touted digital eyewear program, has rarely been seen in public again without them.

Before anyone outside the company could actually touch the device, or see the world through its perspective, the hoopla had begun and has not stopped. Neither has the controversy.

Google Glass is the flagship contextual device. It is the first consumer electronics gadget that uses a new kind of infrared eye sensor that watches your pupil. Thus, it knows where you look.

Over the next few years, Google plans to build a new kind of context-aware operating system around Glass and its sensors. In other words, the operating system will make use of the device's awareness of your location, activity and implied intention. It will know whether you are walking, running, skiing, biking, shopping or driving, and tailor information to you accordingly. But that's a future development. Google spent most of 2013 building and testing Glass, in full public view.

Google, usually tight-lipped before products are launched, started titillating the public with juicy previews. At a developer conference in June 2012, nine months prior to releasing an Explorer version to technologists, skydivers leapt from a blimp[†††] over San Francisco, demonstrating what the city looks like as you hurtle through the air to a designated landing area.

A month later, Project Glass converged with Project Runway at a tony Manhattan fashion show where models paraded wearing the sleek devices and expensive couture. The company understood that if Glass is to be worn on the face, it has to be perceived as fashionable.

Brin started speaking publicly with far greater frequency than is his habit. He was seen riding in a New York City subway wearing the device. The company produced periodic videos on its YouTube property showing how productive and enjoyable life through Glass could be.

But that was all concept. Some of what was promised in advance was no more real in the early stages of public scrutiny than a little girl's fantasy that she could follow a hare—late for a date—through a looking glass and down a huge hole in a big tree.

The first people outside of Google to touch Glass were about 2000 independent developers, influencers and tech journalists who started receiving the "Explorer Version" in April 2013. It was something less than had been portrayed in the conceptual videos—but simultaneously it was something more than anyone had ever experienced.

For developers who might build the apps that would help Glass meet its potential, the cost was $1500 each, and there wasn't much you could do with it that you couldn't already do with a smartphone. Still, most people who tried them saw great—perhaps even historic—potential.

Many suggested something new you *could* do with Glass. Some thought it would change the relationship between people and devices—for better or worse. We are among those who think it will be for the better.

In the following months another 6000 Glass devices were parsed out to winners of the If I had Glass[†††] contest that the company ran. This group was composed of fewer technical professionals but, by virtue of the contest they won, they were articulate people, eager to be in the front of the line and positioned to feel they had just won—rather than paid $1500. In short, they were predisposed to speak kindly of Glass.

In those first months, however, new functionality accrued steadily— if unremarkably. The *New York Times* reported that you could do useful and interesting little tasks, like take pictures, read, and use Twitter, Path, Tumblr and Facebook.

Again, those were tasks you could already perform on your phone— except a few things were very different. You did all these things hands free. Your computer was seeing what you were seeing at the same time as you were. Instead of typing to instruct your device, you just talked to it in natural language, or used taps and gestures.

Long before Glass was offered to the general public, new and unique experiences were observed and reported. By August 2013 we were attending hackathons where we saw apps that used Glass to play games, fly drones, help doctors and control robots. Unfortunately, our writing deadlines required us to finish this chapter before such new applications became available, before Google announced its actual retail price and before everyday people got to spend any time at all using Glass.

We did, however, enjoy a good deal of hands-on experience ourselves, and we paid close attention to what other early adopters reported. Some shared our unsinkable enthusiasm; others thought less of it. Respected journalists such as VentureBeat's Jolie O'Dell declared,[†††] "This isn't and never will be a good device for consumers." Others were even less kind.

What is unquestionable is that Glass, the first facially mounted personal computing device intended for mass markets, got into the conversation. A Bing search for "Google Glass" generated 149 million results on May 10, 2013, up by more than 125 million in about 30 days.

In fact, we can think of no product, service or media event that has ever become a worldwide recognized brand so early in its development. No product has ever been so craved or vilified so long before it was available.

Many who could draw attention by inciting fear, uncertainty and doubt were active early:

- The Five Point Cafe,[†††] a Seattle neighborhood tavern, banned the device without ever seeing one. The proprietor made it clear he didn't want any geeks spying on his patrons.
- Gary Howell,[†††] a state representative in West Virginia, proposed a ban on driving while Glassing.
- A national petition was started to prohibit Glass use as an illegal surveillance device,[†††] although it did not specify just how that surveillance would be conducted or by whom.
- Jeff Bercovici,[†††] a *Forbes* staff writer, warned Glass would make classroom cheating rampant.[†††]
- Theaters,[†††] where recording or taking pictures with any device is already prohibited, started issuing bans specifically addressed to the new device.
- The *Urban Dictionary*, a compendium of streetwise lingo added a listing: "Glasshole—a person who constantly talks to his Google Glass, ignoring the outside world."[†††]

All this angst was expressed by people who had not yet touched the device—and perhaps never will.

Glass was not the first digital eyewear to be introduced, nor was it the second. It wasn't even the first to freak people out. Steve Mann,[†††] a Canadian professor was enjoying lunch with his family at a McDonald's[†††] on the Champs Élysées in Paris when staff members, who found the device he was wearing disturbing, dragged him out of the establishment and into the street.

Oakley,[†††] the design maestros, had no such problems when they launched Airwave,[†††] high-end ski goggles that feature GPS, Bluetooth and a small screen inside that lets you see where your friends are on the mountain, where you are, how fast you're skiing and even the hang time of your last jump.

So, why all the attention? Is it just noise, or is something new and significant going on?

We believe something monumental is taking place, something that could change your life and work, your children's future and the world in which your unborn descendants will live.

Not Another Day

Scoble was the 107th person to receive a Google Glass prototype. He put them on and immediately started posting short notes on his social networks about his experience. He wore them when he went to Europe, making presentations at tech conferences and letting hundreds of people give his Glass device a quick try.[†††]

After two weeks, he posted his first review to Google+, the default social network for Google Glass users, declaring "I'm never going to live another day without a wearable computer on my face."[†††]

To illustrate his point, his wife Maryam photographed him in the shower wearing his Glass. Some scorned the stunt. "If Google Glass fails, it is Robert Scoble's fault," bemoaned author-speaker Peter Shankman in a blog post. Larry Page, Google's CEO, told Scoble in front of a large audience that he "did not appreciate" the shower photo.[†††]

Unperturbed, Scoble spent far more time taking pictures than posing for them. In his first four months with Glass he took more than 6000 photos—along with dozens of videos—and he had only just begun. He says that's about double the rate he was shooting on his smartphones.

Scoble has built a career interviewing developers of innovative technologies. He is known for both his candor and his enthusiasm. He is said to have a sharp eye for spotting new products with great potential.

But even he acknowledges that Glass is not appropriate in every situation. For example, he raises them up inside public bathrooms to avoid claims he's recording. He also feels uncomfortable wearing his Glass on date nights, in nice restaurants, and so on. "They have a fashion cost," Scoble says.

While Scoble whistle-stopped through Europe, Israel stayed home writing *Age of Context*. He followed Scoble's posts with interest and concern. The idea for the book had been partly inspired by Glass long before it was a tangible product and Israel worried that Scoble may have overstated the case. He worried about all the negative comments being amplified across the internet.

Israel does not adopt technology as early as Scoble does, although he is usually a few steps ahead of the mainstream. He worries about unintended consequences and loss of privacy as well as lesser matters such as the paucity of apps.

Immediate Want

Israel got to see Glass firsthand for the first time in May 2013. He was scheduled to spend the day with Scoble, at SRI International,[†††] the venerable and prolific independent research and development facility in Menlo Park, to interview researchers for this book.

Early in the day, he tried on Scoble's device for about 60 seconds. His concerns evaporated. He immediately wanted one. He might not vow to wear it every day, but knew he wanted one and would find many uses for it.

It took only that single minute for him to understand how such a device would improve his productivity, give him access to information and enable new forms of communication. He also thought the device was fun, recognizing that the business value of fun is frequently underrated.

Many of Israel's friends are in their upper 50s and 60s. He knew he would be chided and disparaged by some—but Glass would be worth it. He recalled how he was kidded when he first started wearing a Bluetooth device, and how several of those who reproached him were now wearing the device.

Reluctantly, he handed Glass back to Scoble, but he didn't share his thoughts. He wanted to see how others at SRI responded as they met with the two authors. Would they be comfortable being interviewed by someone with a computer on his face? Would it change the context of the conversation?

SRI conducts a great deal of proprietary research, some of it for the government. How would people who operated in a security bubble feel about Scoble wearing a device that's being banned from sports bars and restrooms?

During the day a stream of SRI executives sat down to talk with the authors about their respective technologies. The conversation invariably started with Glass. People looked at the device perched in front of Scoble's eyes. They seemed to experience the same discomfort you might feel if an old friend showed up for dinner sporting a radically changed hairstyle.

Invariably, each interviewee asked to try it on. Within 60 seconds each understood how it worked and a smile formed on every face. Each seemed reluctant to hand the device back. As the interviews proceeded, Israel noticed how quickly the SRI folk became comfortable talking with Scoble. Very quickly Glass became as unobtrusive as the old-fashioned glasses sitting on Israel's nose.

A couple of hours into the day, Israel realized a remarkable thing: His eye contact with his partner had improved. Scoble wasn't constantly staring at and tapping on the small screen of his phone, as he was so prone to do. Glass had improved the way we related to each other.

SRI was an easy test. It is staffed by some of the world's smartest technologists, many even geekier than Scoble. Next, the co-authors visited downtown Palo Alto, the heart of Silicon Valley. This would not be equivalent to a field test in a Peoria shopping center, but at least it was less tech-centric than SRI.

We sat at the bar at Tamarine,[†††] a fashionable Vietnamese restaurant. It was late afternoon and most patrons seemed more interested in adult beverages than cuisine. An older man stared at Scoble. He finished his drink and approached.

Israel anticipated a confrontation, but the man politely asked to try on the digital eyewear. It was the same as at SRI: 60 seconds, a broad smile and reluctantly returning the device. "It's the future," the man declared, nodding and smiling as he walked out the door.

The bartender was next: another 60 seconds, and more nods and smiles. Then a couple of other patrons: more demos, nods and smiles.

We ate dinner at the bar as Tamarine became packed, receiving curious yet fleeting looks as people soon returned to their food and drink. This was far different than what Professor Mann had experienced at the Paris McDonald's.

Finishing dinner, we strolled along University Avenue. Walking Palo Alto's main street with Scoble is like strolling Manhattan's Fifth Avenue with Michael Bloomberg. People stopped us every few minutes; some knew Scoble, others didn't know him but still asked if they could try on his Glass and, of course, he said yes.

It was always the same: 60 seconds, smiles and reluctant hand-backs. That's all it took to understand Glass, to realize its potential and to want one.

We heard complaints about price, not privacy. People didn't seem to realize that the Glass they were seeing was an expensive prototype.

Israel's Facebook post the following morning reflected, "[Glass] is the most immersive technology I have ever experienced. It will get a lot better and cheaper. It will change the world—probably not the worlds of aging Boomers like me; but such devices will be an essential component in the worlds of my grandchildren. Their lives will be better for that fact."

Looking Back to See Forward

Please understand that Glass, as it exists, is a catalyst, not a lightning bolt. Some years will pass before people look back and try to understand how they ever could have lived without such a device.

Scoble tells audiences it's like seeing the first Apple IIs as they rolled off the assembly line in 1977: They were like nothing people had seen before, but you couldn't do much with them. Decision makers at HP and Atari weren't interested in cutting a deal with Steve Wozniak and Steve Jobs for rights to market their new computer—the new, highly personalized devices were obviously too radically different to sell in significant quantity.

Yet, it turned out a lot of people wanted them and the Apple II kicked off a 20-year explosion of invention and productivity that we now remember as the PC revolution. Google Glass will do the same.

How long will it take? We're not sure. Our best guess is between five and ten years. And the price will need to be a lot lower.

Although analysts sometimes deny it, all forecasts are guesswork. The future very often surprises us. We find the best way of anticipating what lies ahead is to look back. Let's look back to what got us to today in mobile gear.

In 1940, a device was developed to allow Allied soldiers fighting the Japanese to talk to each other wirelessly in the field. As urban legend has it, a soldier on patrol on some Pacific Island was using the device while hiking past a jungle village. An indigenous inhabitant pointed at him in amazement, declaring "walkie-talkie." The name stuck.

Seventy years later, the walkie-talkie—expanded in capability and reduced to pocket-size—became an essential component of modern life. Sometimes, the best way to understand how far forward something can go is to look back and see how far it has come.

With that in mind, try to fathom just what will emerge over the next few decades. During a visit to SRI, where so many great technologies such as HDTV and Siri were invented, Supun Samarasekera,[†††] a technical director from SRI's Princeton Group, showed us a pair of augmented reality binoculars[†††] that let you geo-tag messages for colleagues and etch in virtual people among real ones in real places. A military platoon could create a very realistic modern version of the famous Terracotta Army[†††] if they wished, or you could tag a window in a building to show friends your apartment, or business prospects the location of your office.

The SRI binoculars are being designed for U.S. military use today, but you can see how they could be used for games, entertainment, retailing, real estate, uber-personalized maps and more. The device today is cumbersome enough to require a tripod to steady it, but Samarasekera says eventually the technology could be incorporated into Glass or some other digital eyewear device.

It may go even further: Seventy years from now—the time it took for the walkie-talkie to evolve into today's smartphone—the amazing capabilities of this technology might be embedded into a pair of contact lenses or be directly connected to your brain, powered by your body's electricity.

Instead of using taps and gestures, perhaps your grandkids will operate the technology by brainwaves, as a University of Washington research project has already demonstrated can be done.[†††] Instead of looking at a tiny screen, perhaps your progeny will watch 3D holograms hover[†††] in the air—a technology being researched today.

Beyond Palo Alto

What starts in Palo Alto rarely stays in Palo Alto. It soon spreads to Peoria, Pittsburgh, Paris, Phnom Penh, Pago Pago and everywhere else touched by the internet. And it keeps happening faster and faster.

As you look forward 5, 10, 50 years from now, the future does not belong to us, but to our kids and their kids. When Scoble brought his Glass to a Mets game, two young kids saw him and asked to try them on, "Awesome," they said. Their parents were less than thrilled.

Maybe those kids won't get Glass for Christmas next year, but what happens when they have their own discretionary income? We think younger generations will embrace hands-free devices so vigorously they will refuse to ever let go and, personally, we think that is a good thing.

Overcoming the Freaky Factor

In *Naked Conversations*, our book on how blogs are changing the way businesses talk with customers, we painted an imaginary picture of a blacksmith at the turn of the last century. He stands pounding horseshoes on an anvil. A few cronies sit nearby chatting and whittling.

Suddenly, there's a loud and unfamiliar noise—a mixture of roar, clatter and sputter. Then, the first car they have ever seen chugs past them. They watch, silently drinking in the oddity. Then they laugh. "You forgot the horse," one calls out, and then more laughter.

The blacksmith resumes his hammering, unaware that the horseless carriage has already and forever changed his life. How could such a crude and limited machine ever replace a horse? How could that crude machine ever become a Tesla? But that is what will happen before the blacksmith's great grandson graduates college.

In 1900 the blacksmith was an essential community member. Communities that had no doctors had blacksmiths. How could they so quickly and unceremoniously go extinct like dinosaurs?

Human dinosaurs are different than those that once dominated the planet. Over the years, our species has grown taller and we stand more upright, but mostly we evolve by building better tools. Our stone axes become weapons of mass destruction; our ox carts now fly.

As British author Arthur C. Clarke wrote,[†††] "The limits of the possible can only be defined by going beyond them into the impossible." That is what Glass is about to do.

Wearing Glass makes us understand how such devices will enhance many everyday activities, giving us new perspectives on reality, adding information and data and letting us capture the moment.

The Specs

Now, let's look at the device itself and what you see when you wear it. The right side of Glass is thicker and heavier than the left. The part that fits over the right ear contains a bone-conductive speaker and battery. Forward, and above your right eye, is the soul of Glass—a translucent visual prism, about the size and shape of a sugar cube.

This prism is where users see menus, read text and email, view content, see command options and enjoy photos and videos. When someone calls, the prism displays the caller's identity, then you tell Glass to "answer" or "ignore." If you are familiar with Bluetooth, the experience is similar but, with Glass's visual enhancement, you don't have to look down at a phone.

The Glass prism, or screen, floats just above your right eye, providing a deep and richly colored display. That visual quality is a main reason so many people smiled when they saw the world through Scoble's Glass. Looking at the tiny screen is far easier than people realize.

The front component also contains an inwardly directed microphone, an eye sensor and Wifi and Bluetooth connectivity. The wide, right-hand stem serves as a touchpad. This is where you tap or slide your fingers to give commands or scroll through content.

Due to battery limitations, the device always defaults to "off." To wake it, you blink, press a small button or tilt your head back. The tilting gesture is a bit odd to behold. A *Saturday Night Live* skit[†††] had a field day mocking this feature. We think most people will stick to taps and blinks.

Two magic words bring Glass to life: "OK Glass..." cues it that a voice command such as "take a picture" is coming.

The microphone is intentionally pointed inward. Glass is not great for conducting interviews or recording an eavesdropped conversation. The quality of non-wearer voices deteriorates just a few feet away.

NBC Tech Reporter Rosa Golijan[†††] wrote that she was wearing Glass in an elevator when a man leaned in very close and said, "OK Glass, take a picture." Glass did nothing. It would be very difficult for someone other than the wearer to fool the device into thinking they were the user.

Killer Apps and Killer-Catching

While some industry observers have discounted Glass because there is no "killer" app, Glass's photo-taking capability already is one. It's not the clicking of the photo itself, so much as the speed of the click.

We have experimented, and the time it took to get our smartphones out of our pockets and into our hands, scroll and click on our camera app, choose the right photo or video option and finally point and click is as long as 12 seconds. When we didn't play quick draw, it came out to 18 to 20 seconds—longer if we left our phone in another room.

By contrast, it takes about one second to say "OK Glass, take a picture." So you can capture an image up to 18 times faster with Glass than with a smartphone. Not only that, Glass photo-taking is hands free, so you can snap while running, pushing a baby stroller or jogging.

Think of the photos in your life you may have missed: your baby's first step, a teenager's game-winning jump shot, even a terrorist dropping a backpack at a marathon finish line. All these shots could have been captured with Glass but missed with a phone. Thus, we think of Glass photo-taking as not just a killer app, but as an app that can catch a killer.

A Very Personal Assistant

Despite similarities to other mobile apps, the dynamic between you and Glass is different from anything you've ever experienced. It makes your relationship with the device more up close and personal. Over time, Glass comes to understand your personal patterns and to anticipate what you want to know, see, eat or buy.

Stefan Weitz,[†††] director of research at Microsoft, talked to us of the day when you will see a shirt in a store window, then blink, or just say "buy." Your facial device will know your intent. It will check the web to see if there are any deals on the item, and then buy it from a retailer you trust that offers the lowest price. It will complete the transaction with your credit card and have the shirt sent to you via your preferred method of shipping.

Very often your personal assistant will anticipate what you want to do before you do and suggest an action to take on your behalf. What's relevant here is that, over time, Glass will contain software that will come to know you better than the closest people in your life.

Does that sound eerie? Perhaps, but it will also be very, very convenient. Your eye-level computer will be with you through nearly all your waking hours, sharing each experience. It will remember them more accurately than you can and will record your most important moments for your future enjoyment and the enjoyment of those who love you.

Mass Market Potential

We don't know what the eventual retail price for Glass will be. However, IHS, Inc.,[†††] a company that analyzes products like Glass, estimates that eyewear computers will retail for about $400,[†††] based on the costs of components and assembly. But they seem to be using the 100 percent markup formula upon which most consumer products manufacturers base their pricing.

We think Google will end up selling Glass at closer to cost—probably between $200 and $300, making their profits from supplemental sales, as razor manufacturers profit from replacement blades. Google already does this with its Nexus 7 tablet. We speculate that Google will derive the bulk of its Glass revenue from the micro commissions on retail transactions it generates. Retailers will pay Google a small percentage each time a customer blinks to buy a shirt, or gets coaxed into a restaurant, or purchases a romantic weekend getaway package.

Of course, it won't just be Google. We understand that Microsoft Blink is developing technology in this direction, and we assume they will not be alone in just a few years from now.

Micro commissions could produce billions in revenue for large internet companies, and they can do that without having to annoy customers with today's intrusive and ineffective kinds of advertising—an issue we will revisit in Chapter 11.

This is conjecture on our part. Google's strategy for monetizing Glass is a closely guarded secret among company executives. We base it on Google's current ban on advertising on its most contextual products. We think the company will be wiser and wealthier if it keeps to this course.

Coming Soon ... Perhaps

In the coming months and years, we expect to see more than a million new mobile apps for Glass and for the other digital eyewear devices yet to be developed.

Many will perform functions already being conducted on other mobile devices; some will go beyond. Imagine:

- Bicyclists, runners, swimmers and other serious athletes seeing routes, competitors' status, race statistics and personal health data during training and races.
- Doctors using Glass to conduct actual face-to-face conversations with patients, rather than burying their heads in the screens of HIPAA (Health Insurance Portability and Accountability Act) terminals.
- Surgeons seeing vital data superimposed on magnifications of the patient's vital areas.
- Police using facial recognition, in a proprietary app, to see the record of a suspect. They will record video while pursuing a suspect that could be used in a court to prove the suspect resisted arrest.
- Games using your facial and body movements for an immersive experience of play and enjoyment. A Glass app that enables you to play Frogger[†††] by jumping up and down like a frog is a simple currently available example.

- Archeologists[†††] and videographers controlling a drone simply by looking and using some gestures.
- Security guards similarly controlling remote cameras. They might say, "OK Glass, turn on GoPro camera 1" to search for a missing child at an amusement park.

Those apps just scratch the surface. We're sure you can add to the list. Just let your imagination be your guide. Somewhere out there an ambitious and capable developer may already be working on it.

Big Vertical Apps

We think Google and its imminent competitors will be focused on horizontal consumer applications, and rightfully so. This, however, leaves huge opportunities on the business-to-business (B2B) side of the marketplace, where opportunities for head-mounted technology abound.

Pairasight, Inc.[†††] an Ann Arbor-based startup, seems to be the first mover in B2B. In fact, they brought their stereoscopic, 3D, two-way, live-streaming, industrial-strength devices to market before Google launched Glass. They are working on deals covering about 35 vertical categories.

We first met founder and CEO Christopher Salow[†††] at the 2013 Consumer Electronics Show (CES) in Las Vegas, where he let us examine a prototype of the company's device. Considering its capability, we were surprised by its simplicity.

A few months later, Aaron Salow,[†††] Christopher's son and Pairasight's launch director, told us the company was in several serious talks, a couple of which sounded potentially significant.

At our book deadline, Pairasight was in alpha tests with a Michigan-based service that provides remote diagnostic support to local auto mechanics working on elite vehicles. Currently, the local mechanics video record a problem on under the hood, then email a clip to the automotive experts in Michigan. If all goes well, the experts send back their recommendations in 24 hours—or ask additional questions, which require more time.

Owners of exotic cars are not often characterized as patient people. Repair delays are rarely well received.

The Pairasight OEM application will allow the local mechanic and the remote expert to use Pairasight glasses for two-way livestream conversations. While the mechanic pokes around under the hood, the expert watches, listens, asks questions and make suggestions. Problems often will be repaired on the spot.

The customer gets faster, better service. The local guy enhances his reputation and can accommodate more customers because cars cycle in and out of the shop faster. The Michigan diagnostic center can scale, because each expert can cover more ground.

Aaron Salow lives in Tennessee, where Nashville is the medical hub for the entire state. Quality health care is available in the big city, but in rural areas quality and emergency care are almost nonexistent, he told us.

However, with Pairasight, a Nashville expert can help a country doctor save a life. The 3D capability lets the consulting physician see far more than a simple X-ray could show: The expert can virtually see through the eyes of the local doctor wearing Pairasight during an operation.

The device is also being tested in South Korea, where Seoul is the medical hub and practitioners who lack adequate training often have to perform surgeries in rural districts.

Pairasight's potential seems quite large. Take customer services. Suppose you want to build a deck onto your home, but you could use a contractor who has experience building decks. Home Depot or Lowe's could loan you the digital eyewear and then have a staff expert help you remotely. A single expert could cover a lot of ground, creating a new after-market business.

Competition

Glass, Pairasight and Oakley are the early arrivals in the new digital eyewear category and each has found unique and potentially valuable ways to take advantage of being first to market. But they will not be alone for long. There are rumors that Apple, Microsoft, Samsung and Nokia are all planning digital eyewear products.

Spunky challengers are already getting ready to join the fray with low-priced variations. A couple of Stanford University students have started Epiphany Eyewear,[†††] which, in May 2013, was taking pre-orders for digital sunglasses at $399 each. They are producing the frames on a 3D printer.

Recon Instruments,[†††] which made the technology used in the Oakley Airwave ski goggles discussed earlier, has announced its own Recon Jet,[†††] a tough but attractive set of digital goggles that runs on Android and is targeted for athletes who will use them in rugged environments.

Framed in Fashion

Being seen in digital eyewear is new and different and draws more attention than users may want. At first, people behave just a little differently when they see you, but as we experienced in Palo Alto, this may soon wear off. Plus, the device will become smaller and less obtrusive over time, and we expect it will become far more fashionable. Google has made Glass as sleek and subtle as may be possible today. They are already displaying a sensitivity to the fashion factor by offering a choice of six colors with such chic names as Charcoal, Tangerine and Sky.

Neither of us is known to be particularly fashion-conscious, but both of us spend a good deal of time selecting our eyeglasses, because they become part of our faces. It is a sensitive issue.

Currently, there is only one Glass style. Google tells us that when it's released to the public more choices will be available, including ones for prescription eyeglass wearers.

Bill Geiser,[†††] CEO of Fort Worth-based MetaWatch,[†††] a wearable-device platform, wonders if Google, a company whose culture is steeped in algorithms and data, understands the importance of fashion when marketing computers to be worn on the bridge of your nose.

In his view, wearable devices that are worn elsewhere may be a safer bet for wearable device makers. "Watches and jewelry have always communicated status and self-expression," he says, so adding digital technology to them is a natural evolution.

"Google Glass works for Scoble because it accurately represents who he is and what he loves. I'm not sure that most people will view Glass as he does," Geiser says.

Geiser points out that people still violate laws prohibiting using phones in cars, because they don't want to wear a Bluetooth headset that makes them "look like the Borg."[†††] As for Glass, Geiser may very well prove to be right, but we think he won't. One reason is that the penalties for using a smartphone while driving continue to increase. In New York, that activity will get you three to five violation[†††] points on your driving record.

Also, Google's fashion model stunt showed the company's sensitivity to the fashion factor. More than that, eyewear itself has become a fashion item. For mysterious reasons, some professional basketball players have taken to wearing eyeglass frames without lenses.[†††] Some speculate it gives them a more intellectual look at news conferences.

For everyday people, many fashion brands market logo eyewear. A brief visit to a local retailer showed offerings from Oakley, Coach, Kate Spade, Gucci and even the staid Brooks Brothers.

There are rumors that Google is working with eyeglass innovator Warby Parker.[†††] Perhaps the next design will come from Parker and, down the line, shoppers will visit their local LensCrafters[†††] for a device that fits their taste, budget and self-image.

 We are optimistic about Glass. Google has shown itself to be a long-view player, and when you are devising world-changing technology you need to think in terms of products for children born today, and imagine what they will want in 20 years.

Fashion is important. If Glass is perceived as geeky, then only geeks will wear it. If it looks fashionably desirable, then it may get to swim in the mainstream. Fashion could be a barrier if Google does not play it right.

Bad for Spying

A second issue relates to how Glass sees what you see: some people may become very defensive, thinking you have the ability to record and spy on them in extremely unlikely ways.

For some reason much attention has been given to Glass being used to spy on people in public restrooms—something that would be both foolish and dangerous. Glass can only capture what's directly in the user's line of vision, and when it does, the prism glows. When you snap a shot, it emits an audible ping. In short, if you use it inappropriately in restrooms or elsewhere, you will likely get caught, and the response may be far worse than what Steve Mann experienced in Paris.

It is far easier to take clandestine pictures or video with a smartphone or worse, with an almost undetectable Memoto[†††] wearable "lifelogging" camera that automatically and silently snaps a shot every 30 seconds.

In our view, a great number of inaccurate reports are dramatically overstating legitimate concerns about illicit data collection and downright spying.

Who Watches Whom?

The biggest barrier to digital eyewear acceptance is neither competition nor fashion. Rather, concerns about privacy and the potential for surveillance are likely to stop many people for a while—and some people forever—from trying smart glasses.

What is rarely discussed is our greatest concern: what happens in the opposite direction. When you wear Glass (or a similar device), it watches what you watch. Data is being collected on everything you look at. If Glass is to fulfill the promise of becoming the ultimate personal assistant, it obviously needs to know everything about you.

But who owns that data and how can it be reused? It appears that Google believes it is the keeper, owner and decision maker. It Google has been collecting user data vigorously for many years.

So far, the company has a respectable record for not abusing it. Despite the fact that it acquired a facial recognition company in 2010,[†††] it has said it will not incorporate that technology into Glass.

At the 2013 Google I/O developer conference, Glass product manager Steve Lee[†††] told thousands of conference attendees that design and function decisions were made to protect user privacy "at every point along the way." We find that reassuring, perhaps even encouraging—but not bulletproof. In its first week in developer hands, Glass was hacked twice[†††] by technologists who did it just to show it could be done.

Even if a Glass device is stolen and hacked—or even loaned to a friend for an extended period, Google could potentially shut it down. A thief cannot impersonate you and make purchases with your stored credit card information. It may sound eerie, but there are benefits to a device being so smart it knows its owner and will follow directions from no one else.

The fact is that all technology is ultimately vulnerable. Theoretically, any system that has been built can be hacked and abused. Some bad guys have great technical skills and creative imaginations. What we can tell you is that a malicious alteration seems less likely with Glass than the warnings of those who have done little thinking or research on the subject would have you believe.

Google may not be anything like Big Brother in George Orwell's *1984*, but it most certainly will be watching you.

Data ownership questions will be debated for a long time before they are answered, Meanwhile the stewardship seems to fall to Google and other data-gathering companies.

What will happen when a government agency wants to see that data for reasons of national security, suspicion of criminal activity, tax evasion or whatever? What about journalists, job recruiters and divorce lawyers? Will we have any say in who sees our data? Will we even be informed when it is being requested for scrutiny?

Personally, we trust the people who run Google today to act responsibly. But the company is not yet 20 years old and it looks like it will be around for a long, long time. Who will run it 20 years from today? Will they be guided more by ethics or profit?

What decisions will they make? Will future decision makers decide more on financial issues or temper their decisions with ethical considerations as well? We cannot answer those questions; nor can the top brass at Google—or any other company, because the issue of data ownership will be one that every modern company will have to deal with.

We consider this a cause for concern. We hope this will be an issue of prolonged transparent debate.

We will circle back to the continuing and complex issue of privacy in the new contextual age in Chapter 12. Along the way we will make frequent references to privacy. We found reason to mention it in almost every chapter of this book.

This surprised us. As the next chapter demonstrates we even found reasons to worry about privacy while looking at a box of cereal.

CHAPTER 3
The Customer in Context

Sometimes you want to go where everybody knows your name.

Cheers theme song[†††]

Retail changed a lot last century. It started with shops on Main Street, where merchants recognized many customers as neighbors and treated them that way. It culminated with the birth of internet commerce, where retailers could scale and improve efficiency without any human contact at all.

Along the way, something got lost, something that is hard to recover in these modern times where you can be a global merchant from your home office.

Sam Lessin is nostalgic for those earlier, more personal times. It might be because his Facebook Timeline says he was born in 1914.[†††] This is puzzling because, as head of the Facebook Identity Product Group, he runs Facebook Timeline,[†††] and he doesn't look too many days over 30. But he sounds like he might have been around in 1914 when he says, "Something got lost along the way, something personal that mattered."

He thinks the very technology that has so dramatically reduced close personal service may now be used to restore it. He believes Facebook Timeline might be part of the solution despite his awareness that the platform's ongoing tweaks and changes annoy many users.

The way he sees it, Timeline is a work in progress. It will eventually allow Facebook to recapture some sense of those folksier days through the social network, where it, advertisers and users can all get to understand each other online and enhance the other participants' experience.

It's a challenge not just for Facebook, but for any online company trying to personalize retailing in a face-to-screen world. The convenience of today's transaction-based retailing is obvious, but if you are among those of us who wish we could be known by more than a data trail of our purchase and payment histories, Lessin and others have a long way to go before most people will feel trusting and comfortable, not to mention warm and fuzzy.

Lessin believes contextual technologies can improve the retail experience, as they will allow sellers to understand far more about customers as individuals and thereby enable them to help people in the same way the hometown merchant once did.

Facebook, like other online platforms, wants to build a system that anticipates your needs and can offer you help at the moment you want it, and then not bother you with anything once you have made a decision.

Lessin is thinking in terms that are deeper and more meaningful than the keyword-based messages currently being pushed at us. His vision has a long, long way to go before it becomes a reality.

Vidya Narayanan,[†††] who works for cross-town rival Google, agrees with Lessin. She's a network architect who spends part of her time on mobile context awareness and personalization. More than that, she was part of the research team that got Qualcomm,[†††] a world leader in mobile technologies, to develop Gimbal,[†††] the leading contextual platform for Android and iOS mobile software developers.

"We are just now learning to take baby steps in helping users. All we can do now is little stuff, such as contextual calendars and maps that understand your preferred route to the airport," she says.

Ultimately, we want a lot more. We want online sites to know how to treat us in the same way Sam, the bartender in the old TV sitcom *Cheers*, treated his customers. When his regulars walked through the door, Sam poured them their usual drink without asking what they wanted. As he handed them the drink, he asked questions that showed he understood what was going on in their personal and work lives.

This is a lot better than telling you what people who bought the book you just selected on Amazon also liked. It takes a lot of baby steps to get from there to the *Cheers* retail experience.

Yet a great many of the world's biggest and most successful companies are taking baby steps at a rapidly escalating rate. They are not just the usual internet behemoths you might expect, but also traditional mainstream retailers like Wal-Mart, NFL teams like the New England Patriots and spunky little startups helping winemakers meet more upscale consumers.

Yes, they collect data on you; they use location-based technology to know where you are and where you're headed and sensors to see what you are looking at. It sounds a bit like the opening line in the popular TV series, Person of Interest,[†††] which begins with the declaration: "You are being watched. The government has a secret system: a machine that spies on you every hour of every day...."

Lessin sees it differently. To him, telling Facebook or other sites information about yourself is like investing in a global data bank, "The more you tell the world about yourself, the more the world can give you what you want," he says.

Still, many people will find this chilling. While we most certainly see why, we believe this shift is inevitable. The internet companies you encounter will know more and more about you and your preferences. Trying to stop your personal information from being collected and used at this point is tantamount to trying to stop a tsunami by standing on a beach and punching it.

This is true for you as a customer in the physical world as well. You will soon find nearly as much contextual technology in brick and mortar retail as you do online. The technology you carry into the store with you will talk with the technology in the store. That loyalty card in your pocket or on your keychain is becoming a mobile technology enabler. It has even found its way into the stands of the football stadium—perhaps the most popular part of this invisible information exchange is that it helps loyal fans get their beer faster.

The Contextual Fan

The NFL is the world's most lucrative professional sports organization. It took in $8.8 billion in revenue[†††] in 2012. But there was a problem: League-wide, in-stadium attendance has been shrinking by an average of 2 percent per year, according to insiders. Stadium fans represent the most profitable segment of NFL revenues. It's not just the steeply priced tickets; it's also the beverages and food, as well as all those caps, tee shirts and souvenir bling.

Where are the fans going? They're not moving over to a competing sport, many of which are also experiencing similar fan base erosion in parks and arenas. It isn't even the economy, which has been treating many fans like a linebacker treats a quarterback.

In fact, their biggest competitor is also one of football's most lucrative allies: HDTV. Broadcast, of course, pays big bucks for licensing rights, but there's less profit in it than getting a fan to come to the stadium. The teams do not share in ad revenues with network broadcasts—and they don't get to sell viewers anything.

Each year, a few more people stay home or go to local taverns to watch games on big screens. Multiple cameras and clever audio let TV viewers see the game better from their living rooms or barstools than from the best stadium seats. Besides, you can get a beer and a burger faster and cheaper, and the lines for the bathrooms are a lot shorter.

Beer and soft drinks are a big deal to the NFL. They represent 70 percent of all revenue during a game, and they provide a high profit margin. So each time a fan gets a fresh cold one at the local tavern, the NFL is thrown for a slight loss on the bottom line.

Almost by definition, the guys who run the NFL are a competitive bunch. They understand that when they keep getting thrown for a loss of 2 percent each year, they need to change strategy.

The surprise to us was to learn they see the solution in online and contextual technologies. Starting in September 2013, season ticket holders were able to see the game better on their tablets and iPhones inside the stadium than at home. Best of all, they could get their burgers and beers faster when they're at Gillette Stadium, home of the New England Patriots, the winningest team in football over the last decade. The NFL is using the Patriots as a test case for the entire league. If it works, it will be phased into all 32 NFL stadiums in the next few years.

The Patriots may seem like an odd choice. For years, they've sold out every seat at every home game. They have a season ticket waiting list of 60,000, almost one fan-in-waiting for every seat. College students who are on the waiting list today may be grandparents before they get to the top of the list.

So why the Patriots? It turns out that in the NFL, the Pats have been the flagship for introducing online technologies. Jonathan Kraft[†††] is president of the Kraft Group, owners of the Patriots, and as co-chairman of the League's digital media committee he has been entrusted to explore ways to enhance fan experience through technology.

Kraft understands both the advantages and the challenges of stadium events. "There is still nothing like the thrill of a live game," he says, "but we realize we have to match what people get at home and then make the in-stadium experience that much better."

Kraft turned to Fred Kirsch, the Patriots' vice president of content, whose job is to use technologies to bring fans and players closer together. He has a history of doing just that. He started his KirschWords[†††] blog in the mid-1990s. It became the first team-sanctioned blog and then the first authorized to live-blog an NFL game. He was also the first to podcast a game. These days KirschWords gets about 200,000 downloads per game.

The Pats keep innovating. They post uncut versions of player press conferences on the team website.[†††] They are hyperactive on social networks and have produced a whole suite of mobile apps.

All this has globalized the Patriots fan base, perhaps more than any other team. Today, far more people follow the Patriots online than see them compete in stadiums each year.

Kirsch contracted Enterasys Networks[†††] to realize the objective of using online technology to enhance the in-stadium experience. The first step, which started in 2008, was to wire the entire stadium, making the Wifi network so rock-solid that 70,000 fans could simultaneously go online and watch the same replay or livestream without even a hint of latency.

This was something that previously had not been done, and it required an expensive and complicated double-density system. Completed in 2010, it is used on average by 12,000 fans at each home game. So far it has performed flawlessly. HD cameras were placed throughout the stadium to provide exclusive livestream footage. A single camera was designated to follow the Patriots' charismatic quarterback Tom Brady during every moment of a game.

This wasn't like checking in on Foursquare. As Vala Afshar,[†††] Enterasys's CMO explains, "The idea was to let fans use their smart phones and tablets to experience things that were not previously possible and not possible outside of the stadium." Gillette's Wifi is intended to give fans a better experience than they can have at the local pub. It also provides video that equals or surpasses HDTV.

By 2012, the Enterasys network was ready for live fan testing. Season ticket holders, and fans in elite seats who bring mobile devices with them, are treated to six livestream views of the game plus replays. They can use the Wifi to tweet or check other games as well.

But 2012 was just the start. You might say it was the year when the baby learned to crawl. In 2013, the Patriots' system took its first actual steps by letting "premium fans" use their mobile devices to order drinks and food while sitting in their seats, through mobile apps that also allow them to pay by credit card.

Food and drink aren't delivered to fan seats. "Football fans are very intense. They don't want to miss a single play and they don't like passing hot dogs or beers to the guy sitting in the middle of the row," Kraft says. So the Patriots have set up an express line. Fans get alerted when their order is ready. They zip up, grab their order, and get back to their seat, missing as little of the game as possible.

Fans can also check the mobile app to find out which restroom lines are the shortest, a concern that can become even more urgent than the need for fresh beer. The Pats use location-based technologies so they know where you are seated in the stands, and which restroom and concession stands are nearest to you.

From baby steps the Pats management hopes to be jogging later in the 2013-2014 season. That's when the Gillette system starts getting deeply contextual. They are gathering data on the eating and drinking habits of participating fans. They know when a season ticket holder is attending and what that customer's buying habits are during a game, so they can start to predict who will be ordering what at a particular moment in every game. Perhaps they will start having fans preorder before they even get to the stadium.

All of this will help the Pats predict inventory. They will know in advance how much of each item they are likely to sell, and when they need to be preparing or pouring. The fans are getting a frictionless order and the Pats are getting a return on their investment by reducing costs and serving their best customers faster.

Besides migrating to other NFL stadiums, the system will also be used for rock concerts and other events at Gillette Stadium. Of course, other pro sports teams will follow the Patriots' lead, as will other concert and conference producers.

Right-Time Experiences

Although some of us may share Lessin's nostalgia for simpler times, we simultaneously enjoy the benefits of these new contextual times. Buying something online may often feel impersonal, but it is also convenient and often less costly.

While there is no equivalent to Sam, the *Cheers* bartender, just yet, contextual technology is inching us toward a time when our interaction with online sites will feel as natural and personal as yesterday's visits to the shops on Main Street.

This is not the case only for online shopping. It can also significantly change our relationships with big brand stores located thousands of miles from our homes. Social networks are part of the solution. New ones, such as Highlight,[†††] the location-based social network based we mentioned previously, can alert a store when a customer is approaching.

On a visit to New York City, Robert Scoble posted on Highlight that he was going to Bloomingdale's to buy a certain brand of jeans. As he walked through the main entrance, a sales representative knew he was headed her way because she had seen his Highlight post. She recognized him by his user ID photo. Through Highlight's messaging feature she escorted Scoble to the jeans he had mentioned.

Although not quite remarkable, this anecdote is indicative of a new level of personal connection, one that uses online contextual technologies to inch real-world merchants closer to customers in a memorable and potentially scalable way. It also shows how contextual technologies can improve a retailer's understanding of who is influential in the online world.

Readers familiar with Scoble would agree he is no slave to fashion. Bloomingdale's could also easily see he is not among their most frequent customers. However, such technologies make it easier to expand and personalize VIP treatment by expanding their selection criteria to accommodate those who are known to be influential in online communities.

Using various combinations of the five contextual forces, forward-thinking marketers are shifting focus away from mass messages and more into what Maribel Lopez,[†††] founder of Lopez Research,[†††] calls "right-time experiences," where mobile technologies deliver customers the right information "at precisely the moment of need."

We've all had right-time experiences—the moment when we caught a home-run baseball from the bleachers, shared a first kiss on a beach, were motivated by a wise teacher or saw a sparkling celebrity as she emerged from a limousine.

Contextual technology allows marketers to give more and more customers and prospects right-time experiences. There's a Mickey Mouse organization that wants to do precisely that for your kids.

Magic Bands at Magic Mountain

Disneyland and Disney World, two of the ultimate family-getaway destinations, will soon offer sensors in a throwaway wearable device.

MagicBand[†††] is a plastic wristband that was awaiting FCC approval when we investigated in March 2013. According to the filing, it is a "smart, disposable battery-operated wireless bracelet, coded with admission privileges and containing sensors." The first name of the user appears on each band, which is expected to eventually replace tickets, badges and passes at all Disney sites worldwide. The device contains authorized credit card information, so your family can enjoy its day with abandon, and free from the distraction of constant requests for Mom's credit card.

Even though the customers and applications differ, Gillette Stadium and Disneyland are using contextual technologies in a similar way. They are improving the customer experience within a geographically constrained area. This phenomenon, called "geo-fencing," is a contextual technique that sets a virtual perimeter around a real-world place.

We think geo-fencing will be used in many ways to create more right-time experiences in the real world.

Neither of us is a frequent visitor to amusement parks or football stadiums, but there is a geo-fence located near us that fulfills one of our favorite right-time experiences.

Wining Tourists

As we wrote this chapter in March 2013, a small analyst-consulting firm called VinTank was starting to virtually erect a geo-fence around each of the 450 wineries that make up one of our favorite destination areas: Napa County, epicenter of the California wine industry.

According to founder-CEO Paul Mabray,[†††] VinTank is "positioned at the intersection of the wine industry and technology." By no coincidence, he and his business partner, chief technology officer James Jory[†††] are both geeks who love wine.

As an analyst firm, VinTank was early and strong into social media, demonstrating far greater interest in understanding what wine lovers were saying, rather than figuring how to use social media to broadcast marketing messages. In fact, it did more listening to online wine conversations than anyone, which made them smarter in many ways.

In 2012, VinTank monitored, aggregated and analyzed about 350 million online wine conversations—about a million every day. From that, they extracted 50 million conversations relevant to brand, region or variety.

This helped them build a massive database of individuals and their wine preferences. By February 2013, they had records on 13.5 million people who had expressed their wine tastes in social networks. In an average month, VinTank expands the list by about 500,000 conversational tidbits.

If you have paid north of $100 for a premium cabernet, VinTank has probably retained your name and the online locations you've visited, which they shared with winery-clients looking for premium prospects.

If you once tweeted that you enjoy guzzling Two-Buck Chuck on a street corner, don't worry. Your secret is safe because they expunged you from the database.

VinTank also has watched what you have posted on photo and location-based social sites. Every time a visitor posts an Instagram shot at a winery or checks in on Foursquare or reports heavy traffic on Highway 29, Napa's central artery, VinTank captures the data on where that person was and what she was doing.

VinTank arguably knows more about individual wine tastes than any other organization, and Napa County is both their home base and their strong suit. They also know what wine clubs you've joined, what restaurants you have visited in Napa and where you bought your last case of wine. They know what tasting rooms you visited and what you posted about each.

Based on all this data, VinTank gives wine enthusiasts a numerical rating. It is similar to how Klout ranks social media influencers, but it seems to be based on more data. It's also in real-time. When you post that smiling photo of you with your friends, touching glasses in a toast, VinTank captures it as it goes live.

In 2011, it dawned on Mabray and Jory that there might be greater value to wineries than just using this data for analyst reports. The closer they looked, the greater promise they saw. Better still, contextual technologies removed any barriers they might have faced to moving from just an analyst firm into a more lucrative marketing service.

The idea was simple. Every year, about 5 million people visit Napa. If VinTank knows where people stay, what restaurants they have previously liked and what wines they have enjoyed, they can predict with high accuracy what wines and places people may be interested in. In Napa, those wineries and restaurants are likely to already be VinTank customers.

In March 2013, VinTank started building a geo-fence around 25 winery clients. They are steadily expanding until they have geo-fenced the entire wine region. Craig Camp, a partner at Cornerstone Cellars, a small wine producer in Yountville, was among the first to sign up for VinTank's pilot project.

"We dreamed about this kind of stuff years ago, but we just didn't have the technology until VinTank put it together," Camp says. "Our wine is priced from $40 to $120 per bottle. We need to identify the consumer who is a candidate for our upscale line, and that is not always so easy to do as they walk through the door." How does Cornerstone separate the jug lovers from those who savor Opus One but would like to find something a little different?

When an Opus One lover is driving, staying or dining nearby, VinTank alerts Cornerstone. The winery sends a personalized e-note or text message, inviting the visitor's party to a private tasting of reserved stock.

This is not just geo-fencing at its best, it's also a great example of what contextual marketers call Pinpoint Marketing—the ability to avoid noise and send appropriate signals to precisely the prospects you want with a deal they will find attractive. We will discuss this in more detail in Chapter 11.

What VinTank is doing for Napa has the potential to help other destination merchants such as restaurants, amusement parks, hotels and museums—any leisure time destinations—to find potential customers and filter out those who are nearby but not likely to be a good match.

The magic is that over time, wherever you go, more people will not only know your name, they will be pretty accurate in knowing how they can help you—and leave you alone if they can't.

This increased personalization and concurrent lack of privacy, of course, is going to be uncomfortable for some people at first, but we believe that will change over time. Marc Andreessen, one of Silicon Valley's most respected thinkers and investors, predicts merchants will understand who you are and what you want by the time you arrive. "Today, this may feel a little bizarre," Andreessen says, "but 20 years from now it will be bizarre if you walk into a store and the store *doesn't* know who you are." At the rate of current change, we think 20 years may be a bit conservative.

Uber Experience

Uber was originally called UberCab, except that the startup kept getting cease-and-desist orders from municipalities for operating without taxi licenses. Uber, as it is now called, is a location-based transportation service that will pick you up anywhere in most major North American urban areas as well as a growing number of the world's major cities, usually in less than 10 minutes of your text message.

They always find you. The driver sees your location because your phone is showing up on her mobile app's map as she heads toward you—and you watch the Uber car as it heads in your direction. Uber vehicles are usually luxury sedans or new SUVs. They are almost always dent-free and spotless.

When you arrive at your destination, you just hop out. Uber has your credit card information and the 20 percent tip is included. Drivers are reputed to be extremely courteous. They make about 30 percent of the fare, far better than at a taxi service, and you get to rate drivers on the app in the same way you rate restaurants on Yelp or sellers on eBay. You can choose the driver based on either location or ranking. But behave yourself—the driver also gets to rate you on your conduct as a passenger.

Andreessen told CNET he wished he had invested in the company. "Uber is software [that] eats taxis," he said. We agree. We think Uber is a textbook example of what we mean by a right-time experience.

If you use it regularly, we think it will evolve into an even better-time experience. Uber keeps data on where you are when you text them. They are building an anticipatory system that watches your patterns and, over time, understands that you have a pattern of requesting a car from a given place at a particular time. They can be there at the instant you want them, perhaps before you even send a text message. On a cold or rainy night, or when you find yourself in a tough neighborhood, it is comforting to think you can get your ride before you freeze or get mugged.

Uber may have originated the idea of letting customers auto-pay for real-world products and services, but the concept has started to spread. The Apple App Store has a feature called EasyPay,[†††] which lets registered users walk into an Apple store, use the app to scan a bar code to see reviews and product specifications, click to pay for the product with their credit card on file at iTunes and then leave without ever talking to a clerk. You get your receipt by email.

For us this scenario presents an interesting twist. Contextual technologies are helping online merchants get more personal while it is helping brick-and-mortar businesses get less personal. We support both, so long as the customer gets to decide which they prefer.

Attention on Wal-Mart Shoppers

In January 2013 we attended CES, in part to see what retailers were doing with contextual technologies. We were amazed at how sensors were getting into more and more consumer products.

The company that most impressed us was PrimeSense,[†††] an Israeli organization with offices in Silicon Valley. The firm has been the world leader in 3D sensors for years. PrimeSense puts the magic into many games, including Microsoft Kinect,[†††] where the sensors read your kid's gestures and cool dance steps.

PrimeSense is adding new contextual functionality to a wide variety of familiar products such as TVs, smartphones, tablets, Bluetooth devices, cameras and autos. The sensors "see" with great accuracy and can also tell how hard you are pressing when you touch an object.

According to president and founder Aviad Maizels,[†††] PrimeSense likes to see itself as the miracle ingredient inside other companies' products. "When you don't understand how something works, we hope PrimeSense is the secret," he said. He showed us a sensor set targeted for mobile device makers that was as small as a stick of gum. PrimeSense sensors also have a great deal to do with what makes Google Glass such a breakthrough product.

At CES PrimeSense was sequestered in a private hotel suite where it showed off what a few startup partners were doing with their sensors. All were impressive, but a tiny Argentinian company called_Shopperception downright dazzled us.

They make spatial recognition tools for brick-and-mortar products and brands. Early testers include Wal-Mart, the world's largest physical retailer,[†††] and Heineken, maker of the world's eighth most popular beer.[†††] These are both mainstream brands that usually don't embrace new technologies until others have tested and refined them. The fact that such established brands are already road testing contextual technologies confirms our sense that the new Age of Context is imminent.

Just like with the Patriots and VinTank, Shopperception's use of loyalty programs is key to customer participation. On the merchant side, unprecedented data is being generated on what actually happens at the "point of touch" between shopper and product.

Shopperception installs panels containing PrimeSense 3D sensors on the ceiling directly over a retail product section. The sensors see what every shopper touches or reads, where they stop to look, what actually goes into the shopping cart and how long each customer spends conducting any one of these actions.

The sensors mask the identity of each user. The cameras can recognize the gender of the shopper, but they don't capture their identity Ariel Di Stefano,[†††] Shopperception co-founder, insists, "Our policy is to respect personal privacy, always."

The idea, according to Di Stefano, is to modernize the primitive way data has been captured for more than a century. Traditionally, a clerk has collected most of it with a clicker and a clipboard.

Shopperception lets retailers understand a lot more. While they may not be video recording what any one person is doing, the sensors provide granular data on what people collectively do, giving the store a deep and wide understanding not previously attainable. Where do most people standing in front of cereal brands look? Where do they reach? What catches their attention? How often do they buy the first item they touch? What sort of incentive will get a customer to switch?

In the old days of the local store, a shopkeeper could observe his best customers and adjust stock and displays accordingly. But for big brands that sell myriad products on millions of square feet of retail displays in scores of countries, it is a daunting task to understand what happens at the point where shoppers touch inventory.

The data being collected is expected to help stores understand customer behavior so they can better predict the likely effect of changes. It lets retailers fully understand the value of every inch of store real estate and how position and location impact customer behavior.

Shopperception enables the world's largest retailer to do precisely that with enhanced loyalty programs that use contextual technology to know when one of its best customers is there. Based on previous buying patterns and the route the shopper usually takes through the store, the customer will get special offers on items he usually buys, or Wal-Mart thinks he might want.

For example, when a shopper touches a box—or merely looks at it—an iPad screen installed on the shelf displays a promotional offer for the box being touched, or perhaps for a competing product. To get the deal, all the customer has to do is toss the offered product into his shopping cart and the cash register, which is part of the system, will adjust the price at checkout.

We think the loyalty program will take on new dimensions in the Age of Context. Additionally, such incentive programs can deal with the responsibility of meeting shopper privacy wishes. People will understand that when they opt in, they are trading their personal data for better deals and perhaps shorter lines.

Some people may not want to do this. If they do not want Wal-Mart to be a place where everyone knows their name, all they have to do is opt out of the loyalty program to keep their privacy—but then they will have to pay the full retail price.

Shopperception is not the only contextual company that wants to watch you and gather data while you shop. The online publication Verge reported[†††] on New York-based IMRSV's[†††] sensor-based, data collecting camera called Cara, which they rent to any retailer for $40 a month. Cara can determine your age, gender and whether you are happy or sad from 25 feet away. It is in use in the Reebok store on Manhattan's Fifth Avenue.

The store is using it to collect data on what customers look at and touch on the shoe wall. The store says it is trying to better understand the customer experience. The vendor says that it wants to put a Cara next to every cash register, ad and retail display in the world.

Back in the earlier times that Facebook's Lessin referred to so fondly, that is what shopkeepers and bartenders did. It was called knowing your customers, and most people loved it. Now, instead of someone looking you in the eye, knowing your drink preference and asking how your work is going, sensors and data are being used to understand you.

In that light, it's easy to join Lessin and yearn for simpler times, but retail will not turn back. Personal relationships cannot scale to global levels and it will take a great many small steps before most people are fully comfortable with the coming contextual age. Those who are already the best customers are the ones most likely to embrace the benefits of context. At every wave of new technology, some people opt out. They choose not to drive or fly. We recall a court case involving a teacher who banned students from using Google instead of libraries, because searching online was cheating. That was less than ten years ago.

The Ice Cream Incentive

In the case of retail, merchants have long understood how to use incentives to gain engagement.

Marc Andreessen, whose venture firm, Andreessen Horowitz[†††] has invested more dollars in contextual technologies than most any other early-phase firm, sees the best retail strategy online and off as something called "free ice cream."

It is the marketing concept that enables you to gain users even as you refine early-phase technology. All you have to do, he explains, is offer something so tasty, cool and sweet that most people just can't resist. It's so good they just have to tell their friends, who will, of course, try it and tell other friends, and so on.

Andreessen is actually a free ice cream pioneer. As a young entrepreneur in the mid-1990s, he founded Netscape, the first popular web browser. To get everyday people to use Netscape, he offered the browser for free. Once Netscape had a lot of end users, it charged businesses that wanted access to those early web surfers.

The approach has worked well for many of the companies that followed—Google, Twitter, Facebook, LinkedIn, YouTube to name a few. Contextual loyalty programs are yet another example of Andreessen's free ice cream tactic because they create right-time experiences for football and amusement park visitors as well as adult-beverage drinkers. Contextual free ice cream is delivered in many flavors and in many places.

Among the most awkward for holders of free ice cream is behind the wheel of one of the priciest of products that is not free. We refer, of course, to the family car.

CHAPTER 4

The Road to Context

*If GM had kept up with technology like the computer industry has,
we would all be driving $25 cars that got 1000 MPG.*

Anonymous, often wrongly attributed to Bill Gates

In 2005, Bob Lutz,[†††] then vice chairman of GM, became the highest-ranking executive blogger. He turned to new media to fight old media. In a 2008 FastCompany interview[†††] with Shel Israel, Lutz said he decided to take what was then considered a radical step because he "felt GM was the victim of a media bias" and he wanted a venue where he could talk directly with the car-buying public.

Lutz would become a regular contributor to GM's *Fastlane* blog, where he often argued the automaker's case. "It unquestionably reversed media coverage of GM," Lutz said.

The story was impressive back then, but, upon reflection, it only demonstrated that the charismatic Lutz could make a good case on what was the most advanced communication tool available in 2005. Consider how the newer tools of sensors, data, location and mobility have changed the game, just for auto executives, not to mention the entire automotive industry.

In February 2013, John M. Broder, a respected *New York Times* reporter often assigned to the White House, took a Tesla Model S, an elegant electric sedan, for a test drive from Washington, D.C., to New England. He had planned to complete his ride in Boston but, instead, it was ingloriously aborted in Connecticut where the Tesla ran out of power and was towed away on the back of a truck. He photographed the power-sapped Tesla and reported having had a very bad experience in his *Times* review.[†††]

Like Lutz, Elon Musk, Tesla founder and CEO, chose to blog his side of the story. Although Lutz had to count on his own credibility and persuasive abilities when writing his blog, Musk had a credible eyewitness to everything that happened between Broder and the Tesla. Like most luxury cars today, the Tesla collects and stores data on where it has been and what happened to it in a little-known device called an Event Data Recorder (EDR].[†††]

The EDR is similar to the black box on an airplane. EDRs are being popularized by free ice cream offers. Progressive Insurance offers customers a discount if they install one and allow the insurer to access data. The National Highway Safety Council is lobbying to make them mandatory in new cars. Most people seem to be unaware that they exist.[†††]

The question is not yet settled by a court ruling, but the general legal consensus is that police will be able to subpoena car logs the same way they now subpoena phone records. An EDR can prove where a car resembling the one in a bank surveillance video was at the time of a heist.

Musk used the Tesla EDR to provide forensic evidence of Broder's road trip. He posted graphs that showed wide variations between what Broder reported and what the car recorded. Musk charged that Broder "did not factually represent Tesla technology" and that "Broder worked very hard to force our car to stop running."[†††]

Margaret Sullivan, as public editor of the de facto Op-Ed page ombudsman for the *Times*, concluded that Broder's review contained "problems with precision and judgment."[†††]

"Today's car is entirely different than the product of just five years ago," says K. Venkatesh Prasad, senior technical leader for Ford Open Innovation and a member of the Ford Technology Advisory Board. "Today, the car is a cognitive device."[†††]

Many people do not yet realize it, but the modern car is as much a contextual tool as a smart phone is—only a lot bigger.

Not only can it defend itself against harsh critics, but it can also protect its passengers from hazards and inconvenience, all while keeping them connected and entertained. As Broder painfully learned, today's cars keep logs of their performance and understand the behavior of each of its regular drivers.

Cars have become personal. And they get to know you better over time. They not only adjust seat positions and mirrors automatically, but soon they'll also know your preferences in music, service stations, dining spots and hotels. They know your usual routes, in the context of time and day of the week. They know when you are headed home, and soon they'll be able to remind you to stop at the market to get a dessert for dinner.

In a significant advance, cars are also starting to talk with each other in ways that may prevent collisions. Sensors will soon be used to detect if you have been drinking alcohol excessively and advise against driving or perhaps prevent you from operating your own vehicle. In the future, the car may navigate itself home while the driver sleeps it off. Some cars will have features that protect themselves from thieves—and even certain family members.

Fellow Travelers

We spoke to a lot of automotive people, including authorized representatives at Toyota, Audi, Mercedes, Ford, GM, Volkswagen, Lexus and Tesla. As an industry, they are all headed down the contextual highway. They are all embracing each of our five forces and are investing many millions of dollars in contextual cars. All new cars, even low-end models, will soon have a broad array of contextual functionality.

Reasons for these changes range from safety to the changing lifestyle of younger generations, who want their cars integrated with their mobile phones and wearable devices—if they want cars at all.

Everywhere we looked we saw sensors—and in many cases, we assume, they saw us. Masumi Nagai, group vice president of the eToyota[†††] Division of North America, says the average Toyota contains about 200 sensors and he predicts the number will continue to increase. "Sensors make cars smarter and passengers safer," he says.

Sensors today play a role in just about all aspects of a car's performance, safety and security. They report when your tires are low and when you need maintenance. In some cars they warn when objects are in your blind spots; they sense water on windshields and start wipers at the appropriate speed. They help some cars to self-park, and some warn when you are drifting over lane markers.

Sensors, without question, save lives. They make the modern contextual car smart enough to act before drivers are even aware of small or life-threatening changes. They can tell if leaves, a darting child or a turning vehicle are the cause of a shadow crossing your car's path.

Crash Prevention

The ability to see what's around a car in any direction can save lives, as Vic Gundotra, a Google senior vice president dramatically learned. He was driving his 2010 S Class Mercedes-Benz at 45 mph on a chilly morning in January 2011, when, as he related it in a Mercedes video ad, "I turned for a very brief moment. I never saw my traffic lane stop."[†††]

Gundotra heard a few little beeps as his Mercedes took over its own braking system and brought the car to a full skid-free halt—just inches behind the bumper of the car in front of him. He was unhurt, as were the people whose car he nearly struck. His car performed faster than he could possibly have, he said.

Most new luxury cars have similar advanced features. Historically, as they get refined, these enhancements become less expensive. It is only a matter of time, we think, before anti-collision systems are standard equipment on every car. In some places, governments may require them, or insurance carriers may give car owners incentives to buy cars that feature them.

Both of Scoble's cars, a 2010 Toyota Prius and a 2011 Sienna, have front-facing, phase-detection radar. He says he'll never own another car without it. He, too, believes these devices have saved him from serious problems. Not only are sensors faster than drivers, they are also smarter than thieves.

Carjack Pooled

Nothing might look more tempting to a car thief than a nice, shiny new Tesla parked at the curb or in the shadows of a parking garage. These guys have tools that slide down your window slot to trip locks. The best still know how to jimmy a door handle.

Except the Tesla has no door handle to jimmy and no lock to trip. Instead, the Tesla has a sensor in the driver's door that sees who is approaching and recognizes authorized drivers. When it sees one, its door latch pushes out, like headlights do in some cars. If you aren't on that Tesla's A-List, the door won't open for you—short of blowtorching your way in—and that will trip the heat-detection alarm.

All new high-end cars have advanced anti-theft systems, although perhaps not all are as foolproof as Tesla's. If the car does somehow get ripped off, or borrowed by an unauthorized family member, the car can tell you where it is through tweets or text messages, which owners or services can then convey to police.

Sometimes, vehicles can make dangerous carjackers look like fools. That was the case in 2009, when Jose Ruiz was chatting with a friend inside his Chevrolet Tahoe in a Visalia, California, parking lot. Suddenly, a man with a sawed-off shotgun approached,[†††] demanding valuables and the keys to the SUV.

Ruiz almost gladly obliged. He knew something the thief didn't. His Tahoe was equipped with a GM OnStar system, the granddaddy of all automobile remote communications services. The 2009 version was the first to provide a Stolen Vehicle Slowdown feature.[†††]

As the thief drove off, OnStar started signaling its location to OnStar operators, who then alerted police. They soon spotted the stolen truck and began what started off as hot pursuit but, after a few seconds, cooled down dramatically.

OnStar service operators remotely disabled the Tahoe's gas pedal. About 16 minutes after the operators were notified, the SUV ground to a halt. The robber then bolted on foot—running directly into a swimming pool, where police fished him out and then cuffed him.

OnStar was formed in 1995 as a collaboration between GM, Electronic Data Systems and Hughes Electronics Corp. Its first customer was GM, which introduced the service in 1996 in high-end Cadillacs. The carmaker—and its customers—liked it so much that GM bought the company, making it a subsidiary.

Each year its systems become more refined. Last year it premiered video chat, through a dashboard screen. Over 6 million people subscribe to it, paying a monthly fee. It's available in all GM vehicles and has been licensed to Volkswagen, Acura and Audi. It gets a little less expensive every year.

OnStar uses lots of sensors and has often introduced features that other companies eventually emulate. It was among the first to allow hands-free, voice-command technology for phone calling. It pioneered many safety features and can sense that a collision occurred and if your airbags inflated. Then it checks to see if you are conscious. If not, it calls 911 on your behalf, providing your precise location via GPS sensors.

Sensors also can help drivers become more aware of their own driving shortcomings. GM is experimenting with 3D sensors that will see if a driver is dozing.

In the future, the car may also connect with personal wristband monitoring devices that measure such health functions as heart rate, body temperature and perspiration. If you are experiencing physical problems, the car will connect with your smartphone and use that combined information to figure out where you should go to get help.

Other wearable devices have sensors that can monitor blood sugar and alcohol levels. When connected to the car, these devices could refuse to allow the car to start until a diabetic eats an apple or an imbiber sobers up.

All the auto people we spoke with were focused initially on using contextual technology to improve safety and security. From a pragmatic perspective, carmakers understand that people will adopt new technology fastest when it ensures protection for the people and property they hold dear.

Automotive Clouds

The connected car may travel many routes in the near-term future. Each requires that the car gather and store lots of data, most of which will be aggregated automatically, without the driver's knowledge or permission.

Carmakers are forming data storage alliances with cloud storage organizations such as Rackspace and Microsoft Azure. Lexus plans to build a global ring of data centers. In short, automakers are planning to permanently store data in the cloud, and they will be storing a lot more data than you may think.

For end users, this data collection can be useful. Your family car will know more than just when it's time to change the oil. It will understand your preferences, patterns and quirks. Without any user input, it will know who just slipped behind the wheel and will adjust the seat, mirrors, temperature, music stations and volume accordingly.

If you want to loan your car to a friend, you'll be able to give instructions to the vehicle, authorizing the guest and imposing any restrictions related to how far (or fast) that person can go and at what time the car must be returned—or it will turn off.

Ford offers a mobile app that seems designed for remote parental control of kids at the wheel. MyKey[†††] encourages safety by reminding teens to wear seat belts, and it sets limits on audio level and speed. In a future version, we are told, MyKey-regulated vehicles will decelerate in the same way OnStar slows purloined vehicles. The car can be turned off if the driver goes beyond authorized geographic bounds or breaks curfew.

Beyond such benefits lurk many complex questions that no one seems to have yet answered:

- **Insurance.** Could carriers demand to see annual data logs so they can reward good drivers with discounts and discourage bad drivers with higher rates? Progressive uses a free ice cream tactic to accomplish this today, but could this become a requirement for all drivers? Is better safety worth less privacy? Who should decide: the driver, carrier or government regulator?

- **Law Enforcement.** One of the most disturbing aspects of the Age of Context is who owns data being collected on individuals? Tied to that is the question of who has access to that data, including law enforcement officials.

  What about plain old speeding? On a road trip in January 2013, the always-connected Scoble was using Glympse,[†††] a contextual app that lets others see your location. One of Scoble's "Glympsers" remotely snapped a shot of his dashboard revealing his speed at 99 mph. Could police use that photo to issue him a citation? Should they?
- **Civil Suits.** Consider a divorce case where alleged infidelity is an issue. Can an aggrieved party demand to see the GPS record that shows where a spouse was parked at a particular time?
- **Reselling.** Can someone demand to see data that shows how well or abusively the seller drove a car? This would be more useful to a prospective buyer than just knowing how many miles the car has traveled.
- **Revenuers.** Can the IRS demand to see the EDR data log during an audit in which a driver's travel and entertainment expenses are under scrutiny?
- **Involuntary Scrutiny.** In March 2013, Yahoo Autos reported some federal officials wanted to install EDR black boxes in cars to record accident data the same way they record flight data in planes.[†††]

  The Golden Gate Bridge has eliminated human toll takers. Instead, it requires drivers to attach a FastTrak sensor box to their windshield, which automatically deducts a payment from a registered credit card as the car passes through the tollgate.

To catch violators, the automated tollgate takes license plate pictures. Offenders get email notifications and can pay the toll online. There has been virtually no public controversy about FastTrak so far, although it establishes that a particular vehicle was in a certain place at a specific time. Should use of such data be valid for alibis and prosecutions?

Navigating these ongoing and complex issues will likely set privacy and public safety on a collision course. To ensure one could diminish the other. We won't attempt to guess how these matters ultimately will be resolved, but we are certain the resolution, like that of similar issues, will involve time, extended debate and compromise.

States have been debating motorcycle and bicycle helmet laws for almost 50 years. Currently, 21 states still do not require protection for one or both of these.

Wisconsin passed[†††] the first seat belt requirement in 1961. Today 49 states require them. New Hampshire is the remaining holdout. Perhaps as a touch of macabre irony, the state's motto, "Live free or die" is inscribed on all license plates.

Phones at the Epicenter

For carmakers, one of the most difficult realities is the notion that the phone, not the car itself, is likely to be the hub of the driver's contextual network.

Some carmakers have been attempting to make the car the central hub for every driver's personal technology. Some have been planning to establish app stores where they would market authorized third-party technology, thus creating a lucrative side-business. The idea is that upon entering your car you could download new apps and updates to your phone. A few carmakers started offering 4G Wifi for drivers trapped in 3G zones.

After all, some manufacturers argued, people spend 10 percent of their lives in cars, and downloading would be easier via the larger device.

The car-as-hub model seems like a bad idea to us. Our phones are with us nearly 100 percent of the time and most people are already accustomed to using them for downloads. Having a second hub in their lives adds an unneeded layer of complexity and a potential for incompatibility. We think it is far better to have cars that are agnostic as to operating systems and that enable us to use what we already have in the mobile devices we carry.

For example, when we get into our cars, our Spotify.com[†††] music should automatically move from our phone to our car speaker. Google Calendar[†††] already knows where you need to go and it should automatically tell your car's navigation system what it knows. Perhaps Google Maps will just move from your phone to your dashboard screen, where it will eat less battery life and be easier and safer to see. The same should be the case with other mobile apps.

Car internet communication systems are going to need to be compatible with the personal technology of all passengers, or car makers will end up as isolated data silos. If we have to enter and store duplicate data in our phones and our vehicles, it's a recipe for inefficiency and waste.

Our phones are also better hubs because each user gets to choose one operating system to use everywhere. In 2010, Shel and Paula Israel took a road trip, test-driving a 2011 Ford Escape Hybrid. It featured a SYNC automated system that worked on voice command and managed sound, navigation and climate control to make their trip safer and more enjoyable.[†††]

It was a fine system, except that SYNC ran on Windows and the Israels were only familiar with Apple devices. While the phone was compatible with SYNC, it felt like a Windows operating system which the Israels had not used in years. During the trip they had to pull over several times to figure out how to work the navigation system, and even the radio. They would have preferred to have their Apple software seamlessly transferred from phone to car and feel like the system they normally used.

Smartphone and operating system compatibility should be the user's choice, or so it seems to us. The killer issue, however, is speed of implementation. It takes an automaker as long as eight years to deliver a new car from concept to showroom. At best, they do it in three. A mobile phone app takes about eight months.

This may still be an undecided issue among carmakers the next time you buy a new car. It is not an issue that most people consider when car shopping, but it is one that will very much influence their daily experience after purchase.

The Personalized Auto

The good news is that many major manufacturers are abandoning their "cars-as-hubs" strategy and recognizing that the phone should serve as the epicenter of the contextual hub. At least that's what we hear from representatives at Ford, GM, Audi and Toyota.

In the long term, Ford is toying with the concept of making just three basic car models: luxury, intermediate and economy. Each would be stripped of all accessories and users would select just the accessories they want. Ironically, the new program will be similar to how cars were sold up through the 1950s.

Ford's Prasad[†††] champions this concept, but he isn't thinking retro. He's looking at other technology hardware devices. "Apple rolls a million identical iPads off the line, and they are sold to one million people. Within an hour, each is personalized and unique from all the others. We want to do that with the Fords of the future," he says.

Of course, iPads are personalized, to a large degree, by software, and this will also be true of the contextual car. And the collection of software designed for in-car use is growing.

For example, Twist[†††] is "call-ahead" software that sees where you are and knows where you are heading, as well as knowing the driving conditions en route. It sends a text message to your next appointment while you keep your hands and your mind on the road. Glympse,[†††] as we mentioned, is similar and lets you share your location with others—who just might rat you out when you speed. GasBuddy.com lets you find the cheapest gas near your location.[†††]

Nooly Micro Weather[†††] reports uber-localized weather, within .4 miles of where you are and just 15 minutes into the future, preparing you for the fog bank around the next curve on a mountain road. As we write this, it is available as a phone app and the developer is working with Ford and Toyota for the app to be included in cars as they ship. The integrated, automotive Nooly will signal the car to turn on fog lights or the defroster a moment before the weather changes.

Waze[†††] is a mobile app that lets drivers share updates on road conditions in near realtime. With a community of nearly 50 million members as of May 2013, it is perhaps the most robust source of user-generated road data in the world. Google acquired Waze in the summer of 2013 for just under $1 billion.

After Hurricane Sandy devastated the Northeast in late October 2012, northern New Jersey motorists were frustrated because service stations were randomly opened or closed. FEMA asked Waze for help. The startup turned to its community of New Jersey motorists to share which stations were operating, significantly easing one of the many problems created by the storm.

Take My Car—Not My Phone!

The final, and most significant, reason for carmakers to recognize the phone's rightful place at the center of the contextual universe is that it is increasingly central to the lives of future customers.

According to the *New York Times,* American teens prefer owning a smartphone to a car.[†††] We found confirmation of this trend wherever we looked and believe it is one that people thinking about the next few years and decades should consider.

Back in 1978, 92 percent of all 16-year-olds in the United States had a driver's license or learner's permit. By 2008, it was only 77 percent. Even more interesting, kids who do have cars drive less. The U.S. Department of Transportation reports[†††] that people under 30 are logging about 10 percent fewer miles per year than the same age group did a decade earlier.

By contrast, young people are spending more time on their phones. A new generation is emerging that considers their phones to be their personal computers. Simultaneously, it is becoming cool to not own a car at all.

Ford is not trying to reverse the trend with an expensive marketing campaign, as carmakers would have done in earlier eras. Instead, it is coping with the "democratization of technology," and following the lead of future customers by investing in Zipcar,[†††] an urban ride-sharing service, and TechShop,[†††] where urban entrepreneurs can access advanced tech tools to germinate new city-based businesses.

A Blind Spot

As impressed as we were with the automotive industry's understanding of contextual technology and its importance to the future of cars, we were disappointed to find that, as of now, none seems to be considering the impact of digital eyewear such as Google Glass.

In our view, a computer that understands who is behind the wheel and sees exactly what the driver sees has great promise. Devices that can respond to voice, blinking, tapping and gesturing seem safer and more intuitive and might reduce the hordes of people who break laws and ignore common sense rules of safety by using phones while driving.

Yet, we didn't find a single automaker expressing interest or enthusiasm for the fast-developing phenomenon of digital eyewear.

Toyota came the closest when they said they were experimenting with dashboard displays that appear on the windshield so that drivers wouldn't have to look down.

We think the new wearable devices are a better, less distracting and more imminent solution. They are likely to be less expensive than a windshield option. They will also provide many useful mobile apps that can be used ubiquitously, while the windshield dashboard will obviously just be used in the car. Software will be easier to keep current. A broken device will be easier to replace than a damaged windshield.

The issues of regulation and adoption bring us to what may be the most significant and controversial changes in car making since horsepower replaced horses.

We refer, of course, to the driverless car.

CHAPTER 5

Driving Over the Freaky Line

People are so bad at driving cars that computers don't have to be that good to be much better.

Marc Andreessen, investor

Picture this: It is not very far into the future and you have just arrived in a big city. You summon an Uber car via a mobile app and a nice-looking upscale sedan soon pulls up to the curb in front of you.

You hop in the back seat and tell absolutely no one behind the wheel where you are going. You buckle up, because the nonexistent driver insists you do so or the car will not proceed. Then, no one at all maneuvers city traffic and delivers you safely to your destination, where you leave without paying as your transaction takes place automatically online.

Even Robert Scoble, a legendary lover of new technologies, says that this scenario freaks him out; yet some time in the next 5 to 50 years, this will be commonplace.

Once people get past their discomfort, they will discover that driverless cars are safer than those driven by people. They are also more energy efficient and don't wander over lanes like people do. The pilots don't daydream, or get competitive with other vehicles or demonstrate road rage because the last passenger didn't tip.

Instead of driving, people will be able to do some work, catch up on their social networks, grab a few winks or watch a video. Millions of human hours, formerly dedicated to driving, will be freed up for whatever activities can be accomplished while riding as safely along a highway as passengers do on a train.

The technology for this to happen may come sooner than people are ready to accept. But don't worry: Government regulators, the economics of technology, lawyers and other time-sucking forces will probably slow progress down until you or, perhaps, your grandchildren get to ride in a driverless car.

It's Complicated

At the 2013 CES, thousands of attendees saw demos of Audi and Lexus driverless "concept cars." Some observed that they seemed nearly ready for production. We learned it's more complicated than that.

Prior to CES, thousands of Northern California drivers had already been startled, while driving along public roads, to pass vehicles with odd spinning devices[†††] mounted on their roofs. These cars usually moved at precisely the speed limit and contained passengers. Normal enough, except that no one was behind the wheel.

These were part of Google's growing fleet of experimental self-driving cars. They employ short-range radar, laser beams and motion and 3D sensors. The technology allows the cars to discern what's around them in all directions and decide what, if anything, to do about it.

The rooftop spinners contain a new technology, called "lidar" (Laser Imaging Detection and Ranging). It's a technical cousin to radar that's offered by at least two companies, Aerometric[†††] and Velodyne.[†††] Lidar uses optical sensors and laser beams that bounce off the surrounding terrain as the test car travels down the road. It sees everything: lane markers, signs, people and other cars.

Google, Audi, VW and Lexus are testing lidar devices, and we assume other carmakers are as well. To date, lidar is the secret sauce of self-driving, but other technologies are also under development.

Price and technology are of course key issues, but safety is the critical one. These auto-piloted cars are proving they are safe. Google reported early in 2013 that its fleet had logged more than 500,000 miles on public roads with only a single, minor scrape.

To demonstrate and, perhaps, dramatize how safe their lidar-based system already is, Google invited Steve Mahan, of Morgan Hill, California, to be the first consumer to give the Google car a whirl.

The car chugged along[†††] at low speeds on streets cordoned off by local police. In this controlled environment, the car worked perfectly, carrying Mahan to a local Taco Bell, where it backed easily into a parallel parking space. Then it brought him to the cleaners where he picked up his laundry and drove him back home.

Mahan sat behind the wheel, but he did not drive, which would have been unsafe indeed. He's legally blind. For him such a car has no freaky factor. He wants one as soon as he can get it. He told a news reporter[†††] that such a car "would change my life."

This, we presume, would also be true for many of the other 25 million blind adults in the United States, not to mention people all over the world with other disabilities that prevent them from driving. Mahan represents a group of people who have a compelling need for such a car. They will be the early adopters for this technology. When people with these kinds of disabilities are able to use driverless cars, it may reduce the freakiness that Scoble and the rest of us feel about them.

However, that does not mean lidar is ready for prime time. The devices seem to work fine in fair weather—which might explain why most testing is being conducted in places like Nevada and California—but people need cars that can handle diverse weather conditions.

Lidar is protected by a frail glass barrier and can be damaged by pebbles and other debris. Snow and fog confuse them, and they have trouble detecting road ice.

In 2013, a lidar unit cost $70,000,[†††] down about $5,000 from the previous year. With two competing companies producing similar devices, we would have thought the prices would have come down more quickly. More important, lidar spinners are only a small part of the cost of a Google self-driving kit. We were told the experimental unit, if released today, would retail for about $500,000, automobile not included. We did not ask about volume discounts.

Sleeping Drivers and Baby Steps

Another group of possible early adopters may be more commercially viable, because they could earn back an investment of several hundred thousand dollars per vehicle in a relatively short period of time—commercial truck fleet owners.

Currently, many big rig trucks have two drivers, who are being paid around the clock. Autopilots would allow trucking companies to cut staff. Seeing auto-piloted big rigs on the highway may be disconcerting at first, but in time people would recognize that they are safe, less expensive to operate and less polluting.

If big trucking companies are the earliest adopters, perhaps they would be followed by smaller truck operators such as FedEx, furniture movers and pizza delivery vans. That would drive the price down further, perhaps eventually setting the stage for kits as an option in luxury cars.

All of this would erode public discomfort with driverless vehicles. After all, if it's safe enough to take an 18-wheeler over thousands of non-stop miles, it must be safe enough for the family Volvo to carry the kids to a soccer game.

Meanwhile, the auto industry is proceeding cautiously, getting the technology right and people ready by taking the sort of baby steps that Google's Narayanan talked about in Chapter 3.

One such baby step is self-parking, a feature in many new cars. An Audi YouTube clip,[†††] posted early in 2013 to show how self-parking will soon work, somehow reminded us of the old cowboy movies where the white-hatted hero whistles and his horse comes running.

In Audi's clip it is not a cowpoke but a businesswoman, and she uses a mobile app rather than a whistle. She emerges from her vehicle, whips out her smartphone and commands her Audi to go park itself in a garage. Viewers watch the driverless vehicle crawl up a garage ramp, find a snug spot and into it.

Later she uses the same app to summon it back. As she waits, she watches the car approach on her app. The car knows where its owner is via a location sensor in the phone.

Annie Lien,[†††] is an independent automated driving consultant who was formerly program manager at Volkswagen Group Electronics Research Lab[†††] in Menlo Park, California, where she was in charge of product and marketing for conceptual cars under the Audi, Bentley, Bugatti, Lamborghini, Porsche and Volkswagen brands. She played a key role in the development of experimental cars such as the driverless Audi in the video.

Lien prefers to call them automatic or auto-piloted rather than self-driving, because "it will be a very long time before cars operate without a driver who can take over the controls, except for limited, low-speed activities such as self-parking," she says.

No matter what you call them, they are cars that drive themselves, and we do not feel that less disruptive-sounding words reduce the freaky factor.

Lien predicts the first automatic cars to be offered to the public will come out sometime between 2025 and 2030, and they will be expensive. Widespread adoption, she guesses, would not happen until after 2050— nearly 40 years after the 2013 CES revealed pent-up demand for them.

Lien walked us through a multitude of issues that dampen our hopes that the self-driving objects we see in the future are closer than they appear. To get from a consumer exhibition to general use on public roads will require "a great many incremental steps" in technology refinement, user acceptance and cost, as well as institutional adjustments such as legislation, liability and mixed-use roadways.

Lien predicts that self-driving cars will first be available "in urban scenarios, because the technology can understand terrain and traffic patterns more easily and cars move at lower speeds."

Industrywide, some cars have already instituted features that are helpful in urban settings: Automatic parking features use sensors to back into tight spots without curb scrape or bumper tapping, and traffic-jam assistance recognizes patterns and adjusts lanes or routes for the driver, thus burning less fuel.

Other manufacturers either echo Lien's views or brush our questions aside. A Lexus representative told us automatic cars are "just a concept, nothing more. We have no launch plan," which made us wonder why the company invested so much to show them at CES.

According to Scott Monty,[†††] head of social media at Ford, "Customers still prefer to drive themselves." Monty may have a point. We've noticed that many drivers never use the cruise control function available in many cars, so why would they opt for a driverless feature?

The answer is that most people don't know what they want until they see it. We think when such vehicles become available, safer and more sustainable, the idea of having more time to conduct other activities will be pretty compelling to many.

The auto industry is steering toward the automatic car. Everywhere we visited in researching this chapter, we saw and heard about little steps where cars can now make decisions that drivers traditionally made. Lots of cars have sensors that start wipers when they sense water. Some now automatically send and receive messages to other cars. At Toyota, they told us of cars talking with traffic lights to avoid bottlenecks and collisions at intersections.

Some experts are more optimistic about when driverless cars will arrive in a showroom near you. Bob Lutz, GM's retired vice chairman, predicts that driverless cars would be ubiquitous in about 20 years.

We think it will be more like ten years before the vehicles are technically ready and affordable. In the time it took us to write this chapter, our friend John Markoff, a *New York Times* technology reporter, may have witnessed a technological breakthrough when he was a passenger in a driverless, lidar-less[†††] Audi A7 that zipped down an Israeli highway at 65 miles an hour.

Equipped with a system from a Netherlands-based start up called Mobileye Vision Technologies,[†††] the system could significantly reduce costs compared with lidar-based systems.

During the same period, Tesla's Musk, who has long been linked by investments and friendship with Google's founders, declared "...Google's current approach ... is too expensive. It's better to have an optical system ... that [can] figure out what's going on just by looking at things."

So far, however, optical systems only work on flat and sunny highways— not on city streets. How long it will take to make them safe in all situations remains an unanswered question. Still, we will bet on entrepreneurs and opportunity to accelerate the road to market.

Institutional Barriers

What may slow down the driverless car as decisively as OnStar's anti-theft feature slows car thieves is government regulation and how liability will be assigned.

History shows that public officials are not often motivated by common sense and public safety. For example, as we mentioned, some states are still debating seat belts and helmets after more than 50 years.

Could the process be expedited? Progress makes odd bedfellows: Insurance carriers would love to see liability shift from drivers to carmakers; so would lawyers, who would see larger contingency fee possibilities. Federal agencies may also support speeding up the regulatory process: The U.S. Department of Transportation has already stated it favors auto-piloting, and the Environmental Protection Agency (EPA) might like the reduced pollution from auto-piloted cars.

All this gives us some cause for hope. Perhaps New Hampshire could change its motto from "Live Free or Die" to "Drive Hands-Free and Live."

So why is virtually every major carmaker investing decades and dollars into developing driverless vehicles when it will increase their own liability?

Volkswagen's Lien suggests two reasons: "First, we do it because we can. Engineers see a possibility and they just have to go for it. They cannot stop themselves. It is their nature. Second, if our company doesn't develop automatic driving capability, another company will. No carmaker wants to be left behind." Yet another reason is that it will be easier for carmakers to comply with environmental regulations because autopilots perform more efficiently.

Those who see these cars as 50 years away are assuming that the pace will continue at its present rate, disregarding how technology development often accelerates beyond predictable rates. We believe that government has an obligation to make rules that ensure public safety, whether it be helmets, seat belts or autopilots in cars. The issue is that technology innovation moves so much faster than the regulators. The regulatory gap is likely to cause injury and death.

What we find interesting is the evidence that the next generation may branch into two automotive subgroups: those who go driverless and those who go without cars altogether. That latter group is composed of a demographic group that is growing in number and significance.

We call them the New Urbanists.

CHAPTER 6
The New Urbanists

We choose to go to the moon in this decade and do the other things, not because they are easy, but because they are hard, … because that challenge is one that we are willing to accept…

John F. Kennedy

G reg Lindsay was born in 1977, in the central Illinois village of Bourbonnais, an hour's drive south of Chicago. He was raised in a modest single-family home on the last residential street before cornfields replaced houses.

He grew up unsatisfied in his surroundings. At the time, Bourbonnais had a population of about 10,000 and, early on, Lindsay became curious to see more than what his village had to offer. It helped when he turned 16 and got his wheels. He got his first taste of urban life when he attended summer camp in Philadelphia.

Lindsay left home to earn a journalism degree at the University of Illinois at Urbana-Champaign,[†††] a community he found to be even more culturally rural than his hometown. He was fortunate to land summer internships in San Francisco and then New York City, where he flourished in city life.

Almost immediately after graduation Lindsay moved to New York City, where he has remained for the past 15 years. "Once I got here, I never looked back," he says.

He describes himself to us as an "ardent urbanist," a passionate champion of a city life, enriched by contextual technologies. He's made a profession of it, writing about cities and the future for such respected publications as *FastCompany*, the *New York Times* and the *Wall Street Journal*. Intel, Audi and Blackberry are among the companies that have invited him in to talk about the emerging trend toward contextual cities.

Lindsay, his wife Sophie, and their young son Teddy own a "shoebox apartment" in Brooklyn Heights. "We live in the oldest and arguably most beautiful neighborhood in Brooklyn, steps away from Brooklyn Bridge Park, along the East River with playgrounds, athletic fields and breathtaking views," he says. "We've traded a considerable amount of private space for one-of-a-kind public amenities."

The Lindsays don't own a car. When they need one, there's a Zipcar garage nearby. The rest of the time they get around by subway, bikes and on foot. Each morning Lindsay walks to his co-work space, dropping little Teddy off at daycare en route. To visit Sophie's folks near Boston they take the Amtrak Bullet Train.

"I like the buzz and connection of city life. I want to live and work and raise my family in a city environment," he says.

New Urbanists

The Lindsay family is not alone. They are among millions of young adults, raised in the suburbs, who left home for higher education and then moved to cities where they found jobs, established roots and are raising families.

These "New Urbanists" are educated and financially comfortable. They are more connected to their mobile devices than to cars and backyard patios. They represent a significant trend that is accelerating the transition into this new Age of Context.

They are changing the character and flavor of their cities, and their concerns for raising children are helping them lead charges for safer streets and better education where contextual tools play a part.

These New Urbanists reverse a trend followed by each generation since the end of World War II. For more than 60 years, people migrated out of cities, into suburbs. Today, instead of opting for freestanding single-family homes surrounded by lawns, fences and chirping birds, this emerging generation is massively opting for less pastoral—and more stimulating—urban settings.

New Urbanism is changing American demographic trends. Multiple reports, including those from the U.S. Census Bureau and the Brookings Institution, see multiyear trends where cities are growing younger and more affluent, while suburbs are shrinking, aging and experiencing increases in poverty.[†††]

New Urbanists lead contextual lives in cities being planned, designed and rebuilt with contextual technologies. There are tens of millions of them, and their numbers are growing.

Mobile devices, along with sensors, data, location and social networks, are essential to how New Urbanists will work, raise families, use transportation, shop, communicate, learn, stay healthy and even influence government and politics in the coming years.

Few own cars or want to. Like the Lindsays, they walk, use bikes, scooters, skateboards, public transit and shared car services.

Lindsay maintains that the urban boom would not be possible without the contextual forces. "I see a direct line between the downfall of the car and the rise of connected technology," he says. "You no longer have to cruise to find somebody. We now have social media to find people who interest us. This is what tilted the balance to the city for my generation."

This, of course, will significantly change cities over the next generation or two—perhaps longer. The New Urbanists will expect, and get, more from municipal governments. Cloud-based technologies will make it inexpensive and easy for governments to disseminate information widely and to facilitate scalable conversations with their constituencies. In fact, they already do.

Of course, we have a long way to go before we attain a truly open, responsive government. However, when we look at a few forward-thinking municipal governments we see glimmers of hope.

New Urbanists are active proponents of safer streets, reduced pollution, transparent government and neighborhood activism. They are using contextual technologies as power tools for change.

Their shopping—even when local—is becoming mobile device-centric. They are encouraging and adopting new services that allow local merchants to deliver goods to urban doors.

New Urbanism is not only taking hold in such cultural centers as New York and San Francisco, but also in previously forsaken places like Pittsburgh, Detroit and Youngstown, Ohio,[†††] which is reporting a significant growth in young adults, spawned in part by a tech center that employs more than 300 people, mostly recent college grads. Even Cleveland, which in 2010 was voted America's most miserable city,[†††] is enjoying a resurgence of energy from this desirable demographic.

Allison Peltz,[†††] 30, raised and educated in suburban Ohio, moved into Cleveland when she took an interactive marketing job. She rented an 800-square-foot studio in downtown Cleveland in 2011.

"Cleveland is booming," she reports. "There's a sense of community downtown. My neighbors and I look to the streets and parks as our backyards and playgrounds. We support local businesses."

New Urbanists are driving cities into a Renaissance. A great deal of energy and activity is going into the development of theater, music, crafts fairs, farmers markets and nightlife.

However, there is a very significant catch to all this: urban infrastructure. Many of America's cities are crumbling from old age and neglect. Estimates to repair the country's roads, bridges and buildings run as high as $3.6 trillion,[†††] and most of the infrastructure needing repair is in or around urban centers.

Many new infrastructure projects are being completed on time and even under budget, which is almost unprecedented in recent urban history. At the core of this change are two contextual technologies: open cloud and 3D modeling.

Cloud-Based Government

Open cloud and 3D modeling help New Urbanists see the future of their cities and simultaneously have a say in their development.

Let's start with access. All sorts of municipal plans, records and urban modeling are being moved from locked vaults into the open cloud, where citizens can access far more than ever before and they can do it on mobile apps.

Compare that with the traditional way of finding public information. Formerly, a citizen had to spend an afternoon entombed in the Hall of Records poring over blueprints, thick manila folders and microfilm.

Now, new developments are built in 3D models, where anyone can see an urban plan as it will stand on the ground—and below it. Citizens can see how a new development will impact surrounding areas. They can understand how lowering an elevated stretch of highway into a tunnel will provide new open spaces and let formerly isolated neighborhoods connect and interact. Of course, physical models will still be put on display, but it's much more convenient to view the renderings online whenever you want.

All this clarity and access make it easier for people to see what buildings are being proposed, anticipate how those plans will change their lives and give feedback during the planning stage, before ground is broken.

Several municipal officials told us it is better to serve as a collaborator than as an authority. "If it's government by collaboration, all sides win," says Jonathan Mark,[†††] former GIS and CADD services manager for Vancouver, British Columbia. "New technologies allow all stakeholders to participate in planning and, with the new 3D modeling, all parties can see what the future looks like."

Mark broadened our concept of contextual technology. Until we dug into it, we regarded predictive technologies to be just about human behavior. But 3D modeling lets people regard their communities as living, breathing, moving things—ecosystems where the health of any one part impacts all the other parts. It's difficult to grasp that concept when studying a blueprint, but it is readily evident in a 3D model.

The 3D models let all parties understand how a single, small adjustment can impact traffic and shopping patterns or create possible disruptions to school or safety. They make it easy to forecast what will happen if a city is hit by a catastrophic storm, earthquake or flood.

These predictive capabilities help first responders plan rescue operations. Educators can see where young families are moving and forecast when and where new schools will be needed. Retailers and healthcare professionals can see where new shops and offices are likely to flourish.

These first-ever omnibus views of urban plans provide a path to better communications, collaboration and trust among government officials, contractors and constituents. History shows that relationships between these disparate groups have a great deal of room for improvement.

We do not argue that 3D modeling is a panacea, but we do say that it creates a better platform and a more positive starting point.

Modeling Cities

As New Urbanists increase in number and influence and become civic forces to be reckoned with, the cities they inhabit will continue to face daunting and messy issues worsened by years of neglect.

In these tough times, it can be chilling to realize the jaw-dropping costs of modernization. It's a good news/bad news package: good because spending boosts the economy by creating jobs and supporting local suppliers, bad because such massive urban projects have well-documented histories of corruption, shoddy workmanship and financial mismanagement.

A recent example of financial mismanagement and possibly corruption was the fiasco known as the Big Dig.[†††] Designed to hide a small but unsightly and congested stretch of highway in central Boston, the Big Dig was projected to cost $2.8 billion and take ten years to build when it began in 1982. Twenty-five years and approximately $22 billion later, it stands as a case study of what to avoid in public works projects. Many people are, thus, justifiably jaded about redevelopment.

Nearly every major city in North America has multiple ongoing modernization projects. The hope is that 3D modeling will produce less-flawed results. Cloud-based technologies can increase transparency and, hopefully, facilitate less corrupt processes.

Lately, in cities like Seattle, San Francisco, Memphis, Vancouver, Orlando, Miami and Chattanooga, urban projects have been coming in on time and within budget and have proven to fulfill the promises of program advocates. The resulting developments look and function as expected, and they are less disruptive to surrounding areas.

Autodesk[†††] is a world leader in 3D design software for entertainment, manufacturing, engineering, construction and civil infrastructure. Their software was used in the planning, designing and modeling of most of the urban projects we looked at.

Doug Eberhard,[†††] senior director of Architecture Engineering Construction (AEC) sales development at Autodesk, explains that 3D modeling tools allow large developments to be built the way smaller carpentry projects used to be conducted. "There is an old contractor's saying: 'Build it once. Build it right.' For too many years, urban developers seemed to be saying 'build it once, then repair it often because there's money in it,'" says Eberhard. "That has really changed. There is more collaboration in the planning phase and fewer mistakes in the results."

Urban designers, architects and contractors use these models for "clash detection"—the ability to see a problem that previously could not be detected until construction was under way, such as a vent interfering with an elevator shaft or an underground pipeline intersecting a train tunnel.

On a grander scale, some cities, including Chicago and New York, have built 3D models of their entire urban structure. These models help engineers see the impact of a new highway exit and how it may cause traffic problems near a school several miles away.

Seattle recently had two renewal projects simultaneously under development, one a public roadway and the other private residential, office and retail development.

Parsons Brinckerhoff,[†††] the engineering firm on both projects, built a detailed 3D model showing about five square miles of the city's center. It simulated how the two projects would impact each other and the surrounding areas, incorporating 40 different aspects of the city, including traffic flow, sewer lines and gas utilities.

According to Autodesk's Eberhard, whose software was used in both projects, "Everyone could predict what would happen before it happened. We compiled analytics that could forecast the impact of everything." It took ten years to plan the Seattle projects and four years to build them. So far, all parties are ecstatic with the results.

You might think that 3D modeling is limited to just three dimensions, but time is another dimension 3D modeling software can help make visible. Models can show how an urban area will age over 5, 10 or 50 years. For example, New York City has been using 3D models to predict the impact on subway tunnels of the rising water bodies surrounding Manhattan. All of New York City's data is stored in a single cloud-based space.

Equally important is the ability to filter out what you don't need to see at a particular time. As Eberhard notes, "A first responder needs to see floor plans, understand what's underground; to see where fire hoses hook up, and where hazardous materials are stored. When she or he enters a burning building, knowing where the nearest Starbucks is located is not helpful data."

Perhaps augmented reality can be used in a future Google Glass, PairaSight app or other digital eyewear device to see what's ahead in a smoke-filled hallway. To us, this is an example of using anticipatory technology as if your life depended upon it. What starts as a cloud-based model today may save the life of a firefighter or blast victim tomorrow.

A Smarter Approach

Herman Hollerith[†††] was born in Buffalo in the 1860. He studied to be a mining engineer and wound up teaching at MIT. It is said he tinkered a lot and, in 1890, he invented the first electric tabulating machine.

Finding the machine could count heads with unprecedented speed, the U.S. Census Bureau became Hollerith's first customer. He thought the new machine might provide him with a business opportunity, so he founded the Tabulating Machine Company.

Over the next few years TMC merged with several other companies, one the maker of coffee grinders. When Thomas J. Watson[†††] became president of the company in 1915, he focused on making machines for businesses worldwide. Watson was fond of the literal and straightforward. He renamed the merged entity International Business Machines, or IBM for short.

IBM, the most enduring of all technology companies, has a long history of reinventing itself as times change. It has evolved from making tabulating machines to making mainframes, to making PCs, and now to providing software and services for large organizations. IBM does quite well in its current business, but so do several other companies, and to outsiders each seems to closely resemble the other.

Perhaps it was with a desire to differentiate itself from those others that, in 2006, the company set up a series of meetings with employees, partners and customers called "innovation jams." To see its own future, IBM stepped back to look at global issues, such as population, pollution, economics and health.

The company started examining how its current team of more than 425,000 employees in about 200 countries could use their existing skills to make a better world and, in so doing, strengthen the company's software and services position.

Among IBM's assets is that it understands data and uses it to devise anticipatory systems that predict unforeseen events. IBM has taken that and is applying it to its Smarter Planet[†††] initiative, addressing the complex global issues of health, banking and cities.

The Smarter Cities initiative is now a global business for IBM, with projects all over the world. When they examine urban centers, they watch for emerging patterns from which they can glean insights for municipal clients. Pattern recognition enables them to identify problems sooner, and resolve them faster than their competition.

IBM has already accumulated some impressive accomplishments in the few short years the practice has been in existence. Although the company is globally focused, we asked them specifically about U.S.-based projects. Of the ones they submitted, here are our favorites:

- **Memphis.** Police say that IBM's predictive analytics have helped them identify criminal hot spots,[†††] which allows them to anticipate where—and when—serious crimes are likely to occur. Based on the data, they reallocated patrol cars and other resources, reducing major and violent crime by as much as 30 percent. Pattern recognition also helps police understand trends that previously went unnoticed. For example, they now know that car thefts increase on rainy nights.
- **San Francisco.** IBM's use of data and embedded sensors has reduced pollution[†††] emanating from the city's thousand miles of sewer lines. Public utilities report that IBM's preventive intelligence has helped reduce improve their preventive to corrective maintenance repair costs ratio by 11 percent.
- **Chattanooga-Hamilton County.** The county uses IBM's predictive analytics to understand how adverse patterns develop. This allowed them to identify at-risk children earlier, so educators could adjust personal attention and curriculum, resulting in an 8 percent increase in the graduation rate. One facility, the Howard School of Academics and Technology reported the graduation rate tripling over the program's first six years.[†††]
- **Miami-Dade County.** IBM has helped the 35 Dade County municipalities share data, thus making it easier to collaborate in a wide array of areas including water, transportation and law enforcement. They are also sharing contextual technologies to make government more transparent. A new water project alone is expected to save the county $1 million per year.

Contextual City Startups

IBM has also served as a global recruiter, mentor and partner for startups focused on solving city problems with contextual technology. A few that are associated with IBM to various degrees include:

- **Bitcarrier,** a Barcelona-based startup, has created a contextual traffic platform composed of sensors, Wifi, and "just a little intelligence," says chief operating officer Ricardo Fernandez.[†††]

  The platform gathers data from as many as 20 million points across a city's grid, shown on municipal traffic "heat maps." Managers use the information to reroute traffic, simultaneously reducing congestion and noise and air pollution.

  The sensors replace cameras, increasing privacy and reducing costs by up to 90 percent, Fernandez estimates. Traffic administrators can respond quickly to accidents and other surprises.

  Bitcarrier also improves public transportation systems. City buses adjust so they don't drive around half-empty, and extra buses can be dispatched quickly.

  Most cities cannot adjust traffic signals to accommodate events such as concerts or ballgames because the software runs on data that is up to three years old and can't adjust to current information.

  When we talked in March 2013, Bitcarrier was in use in Panama City, Helsinki, Barcelona, Madrid and Zaragosa, Spain, and the company was in late discussions with several other cities.
- **Libelium,** also a Spanish startup, was a finalist in IBM SmartCamp, a global series of IBM-sponsored startup competitions.[†††]

Libelium CEO Alicia Asin[†††] explains that the company is focused on the Internet of Things, a concept we discussed in Chapter 1 to describe when inanimate objects talk with people and with each other. The company, whose name is Latin for dragonfly, deploys insect-like swarms of tiny sensors called "motes," which report on changes in a wide range of activities that impact safety, efficiency, vegetation growth and sustainability.

It is an open sensor platform that was being used by more than 2000 developers as of April 2013. For example, Libelium technology helps vineyards decide which varietals of grapes to grow based on environmental conditions.

Libelium's main business is creating smart parking systems, mostly in urban areas, all over the world. Magnetic sensors are installed under pavement to determine whether a car is parked in a space or not. The system sees the GPS of a car looking for parking and can direct it to the nearest open spot via a mobile app.

According to Asin, the smart parking system is politically popular because it pays for itself by ensuring that cars pay to park or get fined. The efficiency reduces air and noise pollution.

Libelium's most dramatic sensor effort was in Fukushima, Japan, following the 2011 nuclear disaster.[†††]

At the government's request, Libelium designed a sensor panel that was installed in and around areas suspected of radiation contamination. Each panel served as an autonomous, wireless Geiger counter, which then broadcast real-time information into a cloud-based open network.

Citizens posted radiation readings from their locations to the site, and those measurements appeared on a map alongside values from inside contaminated zones.

"After a couple of weeks, we had a radiation map of Japan. It represented a common thought for people to share and be helpful to all," Asin says. "It's where I came to understand the power of citizens in a Smarter Cities program."

Moving forward, the system will help the country respond faster and more effectively if another tsunami strikes.

- **Nooly,**††† the Israel-based hyper-local, sensor-based weather detection service we told you about in Chapter 4, is another early-phase company working with IBM in various cities.

  Unlike conventional weather forecasts, Nooly covers small distances and sees weather changes such as hurricanes, snowstorms and flooding one or two hours before they hit.

  According to CEO Yaron Reich,††† Nooly can warn cities when weather is about to cause traffic snarls and where accidents are likely to happen. Cities can use the short lead time to make fast routing adjustments.

  Reich sees places where Nooly sensors could even save lives. The sensors could detect a flash flood and underground crews could be warned to evacuate to avoid drowning. Likewise, Nooly can serve as another tool for first responders such as firefighters, who need to understand wind, rain and other weather-related factors.

  Less dramatically, Nooly can help cities save money and provide more efficient services. Although municipal power consumption is relatively predictable along seasonal patterns, cities cannot account for heat waves or frost where quick grid adjustments can save energy and costs.

  Nooly can also predict evaporation rates in public parks during excessively hot days and can adjust watering systems accordingly.

- **Waze,**††† the community-based traffic and navigation app we talked about in Chapter 4, can help cities get smarter about changing traffic light patterns to reduce traffic.

Users help each other route around trouble spots, reducing travel times and headaches. It also helps urban traffic run more efficiently by providing real-time data that can help traffic managers re-route traffic around trouble spots and show the best place to find parking, restrooms and motorist amenities.

Future-Makers

There has been much talk in recent years about restoring manufacturing jobs that have moved from the United States to places where labor is cheaper and worker protection less stringent.

We doubt this will happen in significant numbers or in sustainable ways. First, such a reversal would appreciably raise the cost of consumer goods, and second, most Americans don't want most of the jobs that have been outsourced.

However, lots of new light manufacturing jobs are being created every day, and it looks like their numbers will continue to increase in America's cities for a long time. We were told that there are currently at least a million new light manufacturing jobs in the United States already, most of them in cities.

These jobs are being spawned by the rising tide of the maker movement, a grassroots trend that has been taking shape for more than a decade but seems about to hit an exponential growth phase. It is composed of people who, quite simply, *make stuff.*

Makers are a diverse group of do-it-yourselfers, hobbyists, entrepreneurs, bright kids and retirees. They produce and often market tangible consumer goods that range from knitted products to model planes.[†††]

The movement has its own online magazine and three annual Maker Faires that are attended by an estimated 165,000 people, not to mention the ubiquitous crafts fairs that take place all the time.[†††]

The grand cathedral for the maker movement is TechShop, a cultural, social and inspirational center for those who want to turn an idea into a business with little money and often a great sense of urgency.[†††]

As Mark Hatch, TechShop CEO, guided us through the 17,000-square-foot San Francisco facility, which he said was nearly identical to the other five located in other U.S. urban centers, it seemed to us to be a combination community and learning center, hackerspace and modern machine shop. Everyone we saw seemed ecstatic and busy.[†††]

Hatch reported that countless companies have been formed by people who first met at TechShop. Some of their best-known alumni include: Square, the fast-growing mobile payment company; DODOcase, makers of a bamboo iPad case and other products that took in $37 million in 2012; and Clustered Systems, a next-generation computer cooling system. Driptech, an inexpensive, scalable irrigation system that's used in India and China, was started at TechShop by a Stanford University student.[†††]

TechShop, Hatch told us, provides people with access to advanced tools, software and space. They invite makers to "come and build dreams" for $125 a month or less. Individuals or small teams can frolic in a creative playground that includes over $1 million worth of equipment and software.

Each TechShop facility provides expensive high-end laser cutters, plastics and electronics labs, a machine shop, a woodworking shop, a metal working shop, a textiles department, welding stations and a water-jet cutter that can "slice through five inches of any material on Earth," according to Hatch.

The entire suite of Autodesk Design software—the same tools used by urban planners—is available to TechShop members. The 3D modeling software that can inexpensively create products on available 3D printers seems to be the most popular. TechShop members also receive free instruction on how to use the software.

Like other cathedrals, TechShop builds culture; this one is entrepreneurial. TechShop sponsors numerous events to bring people together with investors, businesses, experts and each other. It holds a continuous stream of events designed to let members share ideas, form partnerships or just provide encouragement.

Hatch describes TechShop as a "transformative experience," where hobbyists evolve into entrepreneurs, who then emerge into manufacturers. The facility helps in every aspect of starting an enterprise, including fund-raising. It even has a direct hotline to the U.S. Patent office. "This is a place to start something inexpensively, then move on," Hatch said.

We met one such entrepreneur, Brian Burling, who founded eMotimo in 2010. He told us that his company makes robotic camera heads that provide "the cheapest panning system on the planet."[†††]

"TechShop changed the game for us," he said. The cost of starting a business using such high-tech equipment has been reduced by orders of magnitude. TechShop enables people to do rapid prototyping and provides a community environment that supports entrepreneurs who want to start a business or use a complicated machine.

Hatch said TechShop users have "an extremely flat demographic. There is an even distribution of people in their 20s, 30s, 40s and 50s. The age of makers ranges from 8 to 80. The only significant change over our five-year history is that 40 percent of participants are now women. When we started it was only 5 percent."

TechShop is a startup that exists to spawn other startups. It certainly is an accelerator for entrepreneurs creating tangible goods, and its thumb-print on cities for the New Urbanists is unmistakable. As Scoble wrote in a blog post[†††] accompanying the video tour, "TechShop is the most important startup today."

We believe that TechShop is building an ecosystem that will be at the cultural heart of what the New Urbanists are doing to improve aging cities.

The fact that our New Urbanists are quick to embrace wearable tech-nology is not just going to put people in closer touch with other people and institutions, it is also going to put them far closer to the devices themselves.

In researching this chapter, we were surprised by how profoundly many cities have changed for the better. Of course, they have miles to go before they stem the blight and deterioration that plagues sections of most of the world's cities.

A bigger surprise was the healing we found in the high-stakes industry where the institutions in control cause even greater damage to people's well-being than local government: healthcare.

CHAPTER 7
The Contextual Self

Quit worrying about your health. It'll go away.

Robert Orben, Gerald Ford's speechwriter

I n Michael Crichton's 1972 novel *Terminal Man*, the central character commits violent acts during blackouts. To cure him, a medical team inserts electrodes into his brain, wiring them to an atomic-powered computer attached to his shoulder. Of course, the experiment runs amok. The patient escapes and goes on a killing rampage.

Crichton's formula runs through several of his books, including *Jurassic Park* and The *Andromeda Strain*. Well-intentioned scientists invent something to make a better world. It runs out of control; people die. The theme goes all the way back to Mary Shelley's *Frankenstein*.

Sometimes reality turns out to be less threatening than people fear. Crichton's fictional vision of electrodes, wires and nuclear-powered strap-on devices has evolved into a reality of tiny sensors, communicating by Wifi to mobile devices and even running on electricity produced by the body.

These technologies don't incite people to become homicidal maniacs. Instead they help people become healthier and fitter. Even though this new era of contextual health has just begun, millions of people already enjoy its benefits.

Although all five forces play a role in contextual health, sensors enjoy a starring role. They are doing everything from helping people lose weight to arming doctors in the fight against cancer.

This is all new. We could find no data on the size of the health sensor market in 2008. But by 2017, mobile health sensors connected to mobile health apps will be a $5.6 billion market.[†††] Its value in terms of lives improved and saved will be immeasurable.

Sensors will reduce emergency room visits and invasive diagnostic tests. Some life-threatening diseases may be stopped before they do lasting damage. Sensors will provide people with greater knowledge of their own bodies than until recently we were even able to imagine. And that data will be shared with forward-thinking medical providers, those willing to become unstuck from the way things have been done in the past.

Sensors on Pills

Redwood City, California-based Proteus Digital Health[†††] is one of several early-phase pioneers in sensor-based health technology. They make a silicon chip the size of a grain of sand that is embedded into a safely digested pill that is swallowed.

When the chip mixes with stomach acids, the processor is powered by the body's electricity and transmits data to a patch worn on the skin. That patch, in turn, transmits data via Bluetooth to a mobile app, which then transmits the data to a central database where a health technician can verify if a patient has taken her medications.

This is a bigger deal than it may seem. In 2012, it was estimated that people not taking their prescribed medications cost $258 billion in emergency room visits, hospitalizations and doctor visits. An average of 130,000 Americans die[†††] each year because they don't follow their prescription regimens closely enough.

Currently, most doctors simply ask patients if they are taking their meds as directed. The problem is that patients sometimes get confused; they also lie about what medications they are taking. One doctor told us that patients don't just forget to take their pills—they throw them out to cover up their forgetfulness. As a result, pharmacists can't detect lapses based on prescription renewal rates.

The Proteus solution gives doctors real-time, irrefutable data on when pills are taken—or skipped. In April 2012, the FDA approved placebo testing. Barring surprises, sensor-pills will come to market in 2015 or 2016.

Sensor-pills also measure heart rate and physical activity, encouraging adherence as well as reporting key data to healthcare providers.

Proteus CEO Andrew Thompson says the system has far greater potential than the monitoring of prescriptions. It is being tested[†††] for tracking tuberculosis, mental health, heart failure, hypertension and diabetes.

Currently, Proteus is the only company to receive FDA approval for sensor-pills. Other pioneering contextual health companies are working on tiny ingestible devices that could eliminate the sort of tests we hate, such as colonoscopies and prostate examinations.

That is heartening news. In our years of following leading-edge technology, health has consistently lagged behind most other sectors. Clearly, something has changed. While the institutional healthcare industry continues to move like a Luddite[†††] with a limp, a bottom-up movement is growing exponentially, and contextual entrepreneurs rather than Washington-based policy makers are driving it. Progress, however, remains uneven.

Wearable for Health

Our earlier chapter on Google Glass and digital eyewear makes clear how important we believe such devices will be. But only a few thousand eyewear devices are being used today and few of them are being used for health-related applications.

However, millions of other wearable devices are helping people get fitter. In fact, health is the largest category of all wearable applications today. Fitbit and Nike+ Fuelband are among the most popular.[†††]

Fitbit calls its $99 clip-on device the "One," but almost everyone else just calls it Fitbit. It measures movement, distance, calories and sleep cycles.

It is also a motivational tool, helping you set goals by sending you cheery little congratulatory messages when you reach milestones. Men complain the devices are easy to lose. Women prefer them because they are easy to clip onto a bra strap where, we are told, it is virtually invisible through clothing.

Most important, these devices have an addictive element to them. Scoble's wife, Maryam, lost 30 pounds using Fitbit. She has struggled with weight loss for many years and had previously tried everything—including stomach stapling—without success. With Fitbit, she has become addicted to a healthier lifestyle, she reports.

Nike+ Fuelband costs about $150 and is worn on the wrist. It is a flagship for the company's growing family of sensor-enabled products, all branded by the +. Other + offerings include running shoes that tell you when to replace them and basketball shoes that record how high you jumped or dunked (or tried to).

All + products talk with Fuelband, which serves as a platform for a personal private health network.

We think Fuelband is a particularly attractive device with an elegant Apple-esque design. It contains an accelerometer and tracks exercise, calories, walking and so on. Some people question how accurate it is at measuring distance traveled because it measures arm, not leg, motion.

The only criticism we heard about Fuelband was that there is no warning before the battery dies, an easily fixed shortcoming. Also, you can't yet swim with a Fuelband—but, as Scoble demonstrated with Glass, you can wear one in the shower.

Users praised the Nike+ site analytics as simple and easy to understand. This is important. Many of the new devices are heavy on analytics but, for everyday users who just want to track essential exercise data, less may be best. Nike says its + family of sensor-enabled gear, backed by a strong marketing campaign, had 6 million users[†††] in February 2012.

The Quantified Self

The very high end of these health-related wearable devices is the $199 Basis.[†††] Designed for "wellness and fitness," Basis even tells time but, with five sensors inside, it does a lot more: It measures pulse, perspiration rate, activity, and body temperature as well as sleep quality. Basically, it provides enough data to satisfy an astrophysicist.

The Basis site lets users drill deep down into personal data mines of stats, charts and graphs. It is a particular favorite of a growing movement, called the "Quantified Self,"[†††] which is composed of people who believe that the more personal data they have, the better they can understand their own bodies and thus become and stay healthier. They track and graph their behavior, exercise, location, biology, genes and anything else that interests them in the belief that the more they know, the more they can adjust and improve their fitness and habits.

Many Quantified Selfers are serious athletes such as Olympic trainers, triathletes, professional performers and competition runners. Some believe they can ultimately reach a point where they just won't need a doctor.[†††]

Loic Le Meur, producer of LeWeb, Europe's largest tech conference, is an ardent fitness enthusiast and Quantified Self proponent. In August 2010, he suggested in a blog post that as people and mobile devices work together to provide highly personalized data, the human body itself becomes an Application Programming Interface (API), meaning that developers can now offer personalized mobile apps for each individual by letting their computer codes talk with each other.[†††]

From that perspective, perhaps we are all becoming like *The Terminal Man*, but today's picture looks far more positive than the one Crichton painted.

As Le Meur demonstrated in his blog, Quantified Self data can build a personal anticipatory system. You can see patterns in your exercise and diet. You can detect correlations between those two factors—plus sleep—and understand why you got sick or experienced an off-pace run.

When Le Meur studied his personal patterns, he saw that he grew stouter at about the same time every year and leaner at about the same time every year. By seeing these repetitions more clearly, Le Meur was able to understand how to break the patterns and perform better.

We don't know if the day will come when people don't need doctors, but we do know this: The day has already come when available devices will help you stay healthier and fitter, thus lightening the burden on the American healthcare system.

Social Fitness Networks

Wearable devices, sensors and data are weapons in a holistic war that must be fought on multiple fronts, including in the workplace and at home, and involving children, the aging population and the chronically ill.

All contextual forces are, of course, involved as well. So is Andreessen's free ice cream, in the guise of competition, gamification, rewards and plain old-fashioned bribes.

Endomondo Sports Tracker[†††] uses your phone as a wearable device. It employs social networking and competition to help users get fitter. You strap your phone onto your upper arm during workouts, races, cycling and other strenuous sports. It automatically uploads your personal data to its online community site, which analyzes your results and progress. You can add music, route maps and heart rate monitors.

Endomondo also allows you to create a social network of your friends, or you can join others who share your activity interests. Participants compete or encourage each other as they see fit.

Founded in 2007, Endomondo reports it has a total of 12 million users and touts itself as the first "social fitness network." Users we talked with on Facebook and Twitter expressed love and loyalty to it, sometimes calling it a "life-changer."

Endomondo is for play, but employee fitness and health is a serious business issue and there are apps to address that as well.

Keas[†††] is an early-phase company based in San Francisco that addresses the business side of personal health. Founder Adam Bosworth[†††] describes it as a fitness social network that helps employers motivate workers to get healthier.

Prior to starting Keas, Bosworth, a respected industry veteran, started and ran Google Health, an ill-fated attempt to aggregate, store and make available all medical records via a secure cloud storage system.

While he was at Google, Bosworth had to deal with some family health-care issues. "I learned that just giving people access to their health information wasn't enough to change behavior," he says.

To help people develop better health habits, he founded Keas in 2008. It provides a motivational fitness system for employees of large organizations such as Microsoft. Although Keas sells its service to HR departments, the system uses word-of-mouth and grassroots techniques to spur adoption, rather than the traditional top-down corporate memo approach.

Keas recruits a few employee evangelists who tell a few friends, who then reach out to other peers until it eventually catches on across the entire enterprise.

Bosworth says the Keas system is composed of four elements: inspiration, motivation, information and—most important—team competition.

Employees form groups of six or fewer members. They challenge other teams and then compete for points. Employers award the winning players modest prizes, perhaps cash, a day off or a free dinner.

Players earn points by reaching health-related milestones: weight loss, a certain number of exercise sessions or distances run. So, being the fittest is not necessarily the most important asset. It's at least equally valuable to meet your personal improvement milestones. Not only do employees get motivated through competition, they also understand that teammates count on each other to reap award benefits.

After five years of trial and error, Bosworth says, he has learned three key lessons:

1. **Be positive and simple**. Tell an employee how much weight he has lost, not how many pounds overweight he is. Keep the data simple, so that anyone can understand it.
2. **Six is optimal**. Bosworth doesn't know why, but trial and error has made him conclude that six the perfect team size.
3. **Social pressure matters**. Keas's data is shared in an internal social community that is culturally strong on competition. The pressure on each individual has less to do with meeting personal goals than contributing to a team effort.

One more aspect sets the system apart. You can't cheat. Patients may lie about drugs to their doctors, but you cannot lie to your co-workers about the weight you've lost. They can see for themselves, Bosworth contends.

Keas has effectively created what is known as a serious game—one designed to achieve a real purpose rather than to entertain. Other existing serious games, many of them in health-related areas, are based on contextual technologies.

Bribes, Lies and Diabetes

Approximately 25 million people in the United States have diabetes and more than three times that number have what doctors call pre-diabetic conditions. The costs in healthcare and loss of life each year are incalculable, because both diseases contribute to so many other serious afflictions such as heart disease, blindness, amputations and organ failures. The disease is particularly cruel to children.

Although institutional approaches have not changed much in many years, a good deal is happening on the front lines of pediatric care, where doctors, parents and patients use contextual technologies to help kids fight these diseases more effectively.

Dr. Jennifer Dyer,[†††] a child endocrinologist in Columbus, Ohio, reveals the key to her successful practice: bribes. She doesn't take them; she gives them to her teenage diabetic patients. She uses incentives to motivate adolescents and gives them a mobile app she developed to aggregate data and help her optimize treatment plans.

She had been working on her system for five years when we spoke with her in April 2013. After much tweaking, she had started to achieve consistently high success levels. She believes what she does in her practice is replicable through a reward-based mobile app similar to the model Keas uses. She has incorporated a serious game as a system component, called EndoGoal.[†††]

A teen participating in EndoGoal earns points every time she confirms on the app that she took her meds, ate right or exercised. The app features a cute virtual pet dog named Cooper that receives a treat whenever the patient takes appropriate action, and whines when she doesn't.

Reaching milestones leads to real-life rewards in the form of iTunes songs, prepaid Visa cards, or retail gift certificates. Local stores can contribute incentive rewards.

"EndoGoal is really just a social business model," Dyer says. "It works just like a Girl Scout Cookies drive. Instead of getting a prize for selling cookies, EndoGoal rewards patients for checking blood."

Dyer personalizes the rewards in her practice when she can. "If I find out a patient likes bowling, I take the time to learn about bowling and try to arrange for a related reward," she says. In return, she gets data that helps her customize each kid's program.

Like patients who lie about taking pills, Dyer's patients can be deceptive—kids these days know how to manipulate technology. For example, some of her teenage patients know how to hack a glucose meter to make it look like their blood sugar levels are consistent and healthy when they are not.

So, Dyer keeps an eye out for corroborating evidence. If the meter says a patient had perfect and consistent glucose measurement scores every day for a month, but the scales say he lost five pounds in that same period, the evidence would imply an eating disorder that had been covered up by hacking the meter.

EndoGoal, Dyer says, makes it easy for a doctor to catch such deception and thus provide a chance to help the patient. The app enables doctors to anticipate the patient's direction and adjust treatment accordingly.

A Parent's Best Helper

Not all physicians are as tech-aware as Dyer, who seems to understand how contextual technologies can help patients forge ahead even if the health industry stands still.

Some parents also understand how to take the lead—while doctors remain set in their old ways. Instead of the formerly all-knowing doctor, Vivienne Ming's best advisor for her son is data-driven technology.[†††]

Ming is not your typical parent when it comes to understanding technology's new capacities. A neuroscientist with a Ph.D. from Carnegie Mellon University and a visiting scholar at the University of California, Berkeley, Ming is chief scientist at Gild,[†††] a San Francisco big data company that helps recruit tech sector talent. Ming's past work involved modeling the human brain. She was among the first Glass wearers.

Both Ming and her partner are big data experts. When their son, Felix, showed symptoms of child-onset diabetes, they did what they knew best: They started collecting every bit of data they could on Felix's eating, exercise and behavior.

The two also researched the most advanced technology for managing the disease. They opted for a wireless OmniPod Insulin Pump[†††] that would work with a wireless Dexcom G4 Platinum[†††] continuous glucose monitoring system. The system, says Ming, is ten times more precise than a standard measuring and dosing system—it automatically adjusts to changes in blood sugar levels.

They also purchased a Basis watch, which they strapped around Felix's ankle. (His wrists were too small.) That provided them with even more data.

When the time came, they gathered up their small data mountain and went to the endocrinologist's office. "At the appropriate time, we showed the doctor and nurse all the data we had gathered, the data that told Felix's story," she recalls. "They refused to take it from us. Instead, they gave us a paper form containing blanks for hand entering just three numbers every day.

"They wanted us to record those numbers for one random week, over the three-month period between visits and then enter those numbers into the printed form. When we did, they leaned over the sheet, squinting at the numbers for a while, then handed it back to us," Ming continues. She insisted that these were capable practitioners. "This is what they do. They just don't know how to handle extra data," she says.

Meanwhile, the couple developed their own app for recording far more comprehensive data. It has proved helpful. For example, they discovered that Felix's blood sugar spiked each school day morning, but not on weekends. Basis revealed a simultaneous reading via Galvanic skin response (perspiration) indicating anxiety. Kindergarten was making little Felix nervous.

Anxiety causes adrenaline to spike, which in turn elevates glucose. A simple insulin adjustment solved the problem—one that the doctor, just looking at numerical averages, would never have caught.

Ming simply created a small anticipatory system that toggled insulin doses up on school days but not on weekends.

How big of a deal is this for Felix? It's life-changing, according to Ming. Elevated or lowered blood sugar levels cause children to misbehave in school. If it is high, a child's behavior can be wrongly diagnosed as Attention Deficit Disorder (ADD); if it is low, teachers may mistakenly assume the child is suffering from depression.

"Our little predictive app allows our son to have a normal life. He can play with other kids, do chores and take a few piano lessons. He can have really normal kid experiences," Ming says. "This would not have been possible without our app."

Ming shared her experience in a talk at a Woman 2.0 conference in early 2013. After her talk, an attendee approached her saying that she was starting a company to create similar predictive systems to manage a blood-clotting disorder. She asked Ming to join the board.

"The point is that technology is being under-utilized in healthcare. So many people's lives are being wasted because they have uncontrolled diseases that could be controlled with available contextual technologies," she says.

Breathing in Place

Like diabetes, asthma affects about 25 million Americans. More than 9% of children[†††] in the United States suffer from the disease. It also seems to cause the greatest amount of suffering among children. Asthma is a chronic disease that inflames and narrows the airways causing wheezing, shortness of breath and coughing. It has no cure.

Asthma takes the lives of about nine people in the United States every day and accounts for one-fourth of all emergency room visits. The cost of treating each asthma patient is about $2,000 annually—for a total of about $50 billion.[†††]

Causes of these painful, and occasionally terminal, wheezing attacks are most often blamed on airborne factors such as pollen and pollution. For decades, treatment has involved inhalers and allergy shots—lots of them. Now Asthmapolis,††† an early-phase company in Wisconsin, has started taking a contextual approach to fighting asthma.

Instead of just looking at what is in the air, it is looking at what's on the ground. It is using location-based data to alter asthma sufferers' patterns, warning them to avoid certain areas and thus preventing attacks and reducing both medication needs and emergency room visits.

Of course, sensors, data, and mobile technologies are involved. The way it works is that a little cap-like device containing a GPS sensor snaps on to the top of the inhaling devices that asthmatics carry.

When an attack comes and the patient uses the inhaler, the device records the time and place and then transmits the data to a website where physicians and public health officials share access. Data is collected from all users in an area and aggregated to reveal usage patterns and to identify geographic asthma hotspots. It provides a very simple solution: Avoid the place and you avoid an asthma attack.

An example of how simple the solution can be is reflected in the case of a group of asthmatic children at a particular New York City school who participated in an Asthmapolis beta test.

The data revealed that kids seemed to use inhalants at the same place en route to and from school each day. It turned out they were passing a refinery where air pollution was high. By letting their parents know what block to avoid when going to and coming home from school, the kids no longer needed to take two doses of medicine every school day.

Asthmapolis provides an unprecedented and inexpensive hope of bringing relief to patients who have had no new treatment options for generations.

Public health officials in Louisville, Kentucky, a city with higher-than-average air pollution, partnered with IBM's Smarter Cities and Asthmapolis to create a test project. The city distributed 500 Asthmapolis sensors to patients. Then it collected data to pinpoint previously undetected asthma hotspots.

Louisville could then inform local people who had respiratory issues of places to avoid, thus reducing suffering and public health costs.

How does this impact the lives of the 25 million people afflicted with the disease? We talked with just one. Whitney Zatzkin,[†††] a member of the TedMed Conference[†††] production team, has had asthma since she was a child. She is an early Asthmapolis beta user. "It helped me be a better patient," she says. The geographic information lets her use medications more wisely and perhaps see doctors less frequently.

Place Matters

Asthmapolis is part of a nascent, but growing, approach to health solutions: geomedicine,[†††] which looks for a correlation between geography and health.

The approach is spearheaded by Bill Davenhall,[†††] global manager for health and human services solutions at Esri,[†††] a leader in geographic information systems. He grew curious about the relationship between health and location after he suffered a "surprise heart attack."

It turned out that Davenhall had unwittingly resided all his life in places where environmental factors were known to increase heart attacks. Despite the apparent connection, no doctor ever asked him a single question about where he had lived.

Although tons of data link location with such afflictions as heart disease, cancer, respiratory disorders, diabetes and other lesser ailments, the medical establishment has historically ignored location as a medical factor.

Geomedicine is a form of contextual medicine. From location-based technologies, doctors can predict what diseases you are likely to face down the line. For example, if you lived in the mountains where ozone layers are thin, you are at greater risk for getting skin cancer. Near polluted rivers? Watch out for intestinal disorders. Coal mines? You face a higher than average likelihood of developing emphysema. Geomedical practitioners can personalize their medical advice, making adjustments based on where you have lived.

Wearables for Seniors

Wearable Technologies[†††] magazine, our favorite resource for finding such technologies, has reported on numerous wearable health- related products targeted to the growing number of senior citizens who are using wearable devices to maintain their independence.

A common feature of all these devices is extreme ease of use. Some seniors have never become comfortable with personal technology and others suffer from cognitive diseases such as Alzheimer's.

Among the devices that impressed us was the Vega Everon[†††] bracelet that uses GPS sensors to set up a "safe zone" so that people with cognitive disorders can walk freely on their own. It also alerts the service if a patient wanders out of the zone.

Similarly, Tunstall Vi,[†††] an at-home patient-tracking device, has a base station that lets patients press one button if there is an emergency situation and another if they have a question. The wearable component is a pendant embedded with a sensor that sends off an alert if a patient falls.

BodyTel[†††] is a system that combines devices for glucose, blood pressure and weight monitoring and can communicate with a smartphone.

GrandCare Systems offers a tele-health system for patients in independent facilities. It uses sensors to report the patient's motion, activities and vital signs to the service. The site serves as a portal for family and healthcare providers to track patient data.

For Whatever Ails You

We were surprised and pleased to discover that at this early stage the contextual health landscape is rapidly filling with a variety of devices able to provide people of all ages with solutions. To get some sense of what we found, consider these:

- **At-home urinalysis.** We found a free iTunes app called uChek[†††] that lets you pee on a strip in the comfort of your home bathroom, then snap a photo and upload it to a mobile app for analysis. Purchase of a kit is required to process test results. Sessions in health facilities involving restrooms and plastic bottles can be a thing of the past.

- **Electronic mesh.** Researchers at the University of Illinois at Urbana-Champaign are working on a tattoo-like electronic mesh[†††] that is composed of sensors, electrodes, and Wifi. The mesh is stamped onto the patient's skin following surgery, where it measures and transmits vital statistics such as skin hydration and body temperature. It automatically dissolves in about two weeks.

- **Unattached prosthesis.** A University of Pittsburgh experiment is studying how brainwaves can operate non-connected prosthetic devices. A quadriplegic woman reportedly used an unattached artificial hand to feed herself chocolate.[†††]

- **Smart toothbrushes.** Some apps improve pragmatic hygienic necessities. Beam[†††] is shipping a sensor-enabled toothbrush that focuses on getting kids to brush more. Philips[†††] is in the latter stages of developing a sensor-enabled toothbrush that will sense tooth decay and text messages to the user as well as the family dentist.

- **Hospital hygiene.** At least two sensor systems are available to help improve the current deplorable 40 percent hand-hygiene compliance rate in U.S. hospitals. IntelligentM[†††] uses sensors to warn health care providers if they fail to perform appropriate hand hygiene before touching a patient, medical equipment or supplies, fostering real-time correction. AgilTrack from General Electric[†††] attaches to washbasins in hospitals and reports employees who don't wash their hands. This is a very critical lapse in patient safety in U.S. hospitals today.

- **Heart attack prediction**. A Swiss medical team has developed a tiny sensor-crammed implant.[†††] Currently in the experimental stage, the tiny, Bluetooth-enabled device monitors blood chemistry. Researchers believe it will predict a heart attack hours before it occurs and be able to alert hospitals as well as the user.

Fighting Cancer

Of the many medical projects we examined, nothing showed more promise than something called FAST (Fiber Optic Array Scanning Technology), which we saw demonstrated during the highly informative tour of SRI International[†††] in Silicon Valley we described in Chapter 2, about Google Glass.

We know SRI as a mecca for tech innovation. Ever since the computer mouse was invented there, SRI has been developing useful technology innovations such as HDTV and Siri, the interactive voice personal assistant now owned by Apple.

We didn't expect to see anything that might stop cancer in its tracks, but that is precisely what FAST promises to do—and soon. The great benefit is that the earlier cancer is detected, the less devastating the treatments to purge it will be.

FAST is a machine about the size of a lateral file cabinet. It enables a two-step process in which sensors search a biopsy sample at lightning speed. It can detect one or two cancerous cells in a batch of 50 million in less than two minutes.

Those cells are then tagged with markers so they can be found again. Technicians then try various forms of treatment to determine which one works best against the cells being examined. As a result of that testing, only one treatment needs to be used in a patient.

The FAST diagnostic scan provides information often missed by standard tumor biopsies. Revealing information carried by tumor cells in the blood, the FAST scan indicates which targeted therapies are best indicated for a specific patient. Catching the disease earlier and targeting therapy may spare patients harsh treatments of chemotherapy mixed with radiation, which are often required when cancer is discovered at a late stage.

Although the process will be used against several kinds of cancer, FAST will take on breast cancer first. The machine was in clinical testing in May 2013. SRI says they are planning to spin the venture into a business before year's end. A production version could be available by the end of 2014, depending on FDA approval.

SRI expects that in three to five years, FAST will be about the size of a home printer and will cost less than $10,000. "We are hoping this will be in doctor's offices within the next 36 months," says Nathan Collins,[†††] Executive Director of the Discovery Sciences Section in SRI Biosciences. So are we.

The Elephant in the Hospital

For all of the incredible advances we see taking place in healthcare, a very large elephant is sitting in the middle of the hospital lobby. It is large, recalcitrant and worse—dangerous.

The elephant is actually part of a herd of regulators, insurance carriers and medical facilities run, not by doctors, but by administrators and bureaucrats who seem more focused on profits than patients.

Why should they change systems when those systems work perfectly well for them and their shareholders? Why develop pills that can eliminate colonoscopies and prostate exams when there is so much money to be made performing such tests? Why should elected officials pass healthcare reforms when fighting about them produces so much grist for the political mill? Systems, when mature, become more focused on self-preservation than serving a constituent need.

"Health" encompasses two parts of a well-known equation: prevention and treatment. We found dozens, perhaps scores of examples of how mobile, social media, data, sensors and location-based technologies are helping millions of people both prevent and treat diseases. In the areas of prevention and fitness alone, solutions abound.

In addition, we think a "healthcare maker" movement is taking form, akin to the maker movement we discussed in our examination of contextual cities (Chapter 6). There is great reason to hope that such efforts will reduce suffering and save lives and, along the way, save people and institutions billions—if not trillions—of dollars.

Now, as contextual technology enters the hospital lobby alongside that elephant, bringing with it the potential to disrupt established structures as it lowers costs and helps doctors serve patients more effectively, we hope that the sentiments of T. A. Barnhart in his personal blog BlueOregon[†††] are what guide the inevitable changes: "It is about people and the quality of their lives." We couldn't have said it better.

CHAPTER 8
Why Wearables Matter

I do not fear computers. I fear the lack of them.

Isaac Asimov

We've seen how wearable devices such as Google Glass and contextual gadgets can help people become healthier. We've even told you about contextual tattoos. Wearables already exist in the form of wristbands, footgear, rings and neckwear. But we believe, as the technology evolves, the devices will get closer to us still—taking many new forms. As they get smaller and smarter, they will perform more and more functions.[†††]

In our view, wearables are the culmination and extension of technology's most enduring trends:

- **Moore's Law** set a road map for devices powered by microprocessors. It derives from Intel co-founder Dr. Gordon Moore's 1965 observation that the number of transistors on integrated circuits doubles every two years. Essentially it means that everything is continuously getting more powerful, less expensive and smaller.[†††]

  In 1976, Seymour Cray built the world's first supercomputer. It was almost as tall, and about twice as wide, as a refrigerator. The top-of-the-line sold for $8.8 million.[†††]

Today, you can buy a Samsung Galaxy S4 smartphone for as little as $129, with free delivery. It is about 15 times more powerful than the original Cray and you could put about 1000 of them into a Cray case.[†††]

Smaller and cheaper means more people can use more power in more ways. And people will inevitably find those ways.

How far is this more-powerful-cheaper-smaller trend going? To the vanishing point, it seems. Some believe that will happen in about ten years. We are among those who disagree because of the important emergent trend, nano-technology, which envisions microprocessors being reduced to a single cell.[†††]

- **Metcalfe's Law**. Ethernet inventor Robert Metcalfe[†††] set forth the theory that the value of the telecommunications network is proportional to the square of the number of connected system nodes. He made his observations back when networks consisted of desktop computers, printers, fax machines and phones. But the law holds true today as billions of nodes are connected via Wifi and are growing rapidly toward the trillions. About 2.7 billion people are now nodes on the global network, and while it sounds strange, that connectedness empowers each of us.

What Started in Vegas...

Where wearables are concerned, Moore's miniaturization is extremely important. If they don't get small enough to be unobtrusive, people won't wear them. Small was fundamental to the colorful story of how wearable computers were developed.

Edward O. Thorp,[†††] an MIT professor whose specialty was mathematical probability, had invented a successful clandestine system for counting cards and winning big at blackjack tables. Growing bored, he took on the larger challenge of predicting the number where a ball spinning on a roulette wheel would land.

He devised a clever system that he concealed from the scrutiny of Mob-controlled security guards in Las Vegas casinos.

Thorp devised a handheld camera disguised as a cigarette lighter. As the ball started whirling, he snapped a picture of it, which was transmitted through a hidden wire to an electronic calculator in his shoe heel which, in turn, forecast eight numbers and sent a voice projection of eight possible numbers to a device in his ear disguised as a hearing aid. It wasn't really a computer as we define it today. The microprocessor was not yet invented and he was using analog components.

Later, Thorp wrote a book[†††] about his experience. In 1971, after the digita age had begun, Keith Taft[†††] got hooked on blackjack after he walked away from a Reno table with the princely winnings of $3.50. Subsequently, he read Thorp's book and tried his luck at card counting but couldn't quite master it.

So he and his son Marty put together a hidden system that included a miniature keypad (which the senior Taft strapped to his thigh) that was hidden under the blackjack table. He camouflaged a miniature camera in his belt buckle. It recorded cards as they came off the deck and fed a clip to a video dish atop a van in the parking lot. Inside the van, Marty Taft fed the data into another new device: a personal computer.

Thus Keith Taft invented the digital wearable computer. We are certain he was as oblivious to how it would evolve over the next 40 years as the soldier in the island jungle was to the potential for the walkie-talkie.

The Casino Fights Back

Technology has continued to play a role in the ongoing battle between casinos and the people who wanted to prosper by bilking them. These days though, the gambling establishments firmly have the upper hand.

Casinos now have their own global network where they share photos of anyone caught—or suspected of—cheating. More than that, they use contextual technology. Every card and every chip is embedded with a tiny RFID-like chip. Every gaming table has a sensor underneath it to detect flimflams such as a player pulling an extra ace out of his sleeve.

That isn't wearable technology, but the sensors casinos use come from former Swiss watchmaking company NagraID,[†††] which has reinvented itself by designing highly secure miniature technology.

NagraID chips make credit cards and loyalty cards smart enough to know their owners and their location. That same technology in the form of an RFID (radio-frequency identification) chip is embedded on contextual passes worn by skiers at Aspen Snowmass,[†††] the world's most popular ski resort, and in the Disney's MagicBands, making transactions for hotels and meals automatic.

Disney and the Aspen resort are among the world's most popular destination sites. We assume where they lead, others will follow.

Of course, that's just the beginning. Service and convenience are likely to be amplified by a few other technologies we've already discussed. Combine NagraID with a VinTank geo-fence and you'll get a new level of personalized, location-specific services or sales, where payments can be automatically authenticated and processed.

VinTank also extracts data from a customer's previous recommendations, so the restaurant, amusement park or hotel can customize its service and offers to each customer's preferences. That little RFID chip and a few tiny sensors on a card will generate a very large improvement in personalized service, and with it enhanced customer loyalty.

Now, toss in one more piece of technology. Put on a digital eyewear device such as Glass or Oakley Airwave, and you'll have a contextual, wearable system that knows your location, your current activity, your preferences as well as what you are looking at in real time.

While such an omnibus system does not exist at this moment, every component of it is currently available. It would not take much to stitch it all together.

And though this technology may be a little obtrusive today, like all technology it gets smaller and more powerful all the time, thanks to Dr. Moore.

One company[†††] is already working on putting Google Glass-type functionality on contact lenses. Today's wristbands may be tomorrow's wrist implants. Down the line the tech we wear may be conveniently implanted directly into the optic nerve where it can more closely interact with the brain.

Big, Soft Market

We expect the market for wearables to be dramatically larger than the current predictions would indicate. IMS Research[†††] estimated in 2011 14 million wearables shipped that year. In 2013, Credit Suisse[†††] said the market would explode from about $4 billion to between $30 billion and $50 billion in the next three to five years.

Wearable technology takes new forms and performs new tasks in innovative ways. And analysts frequently overlook what happens as one generation comes of age, displacing another. It seems inevitable to us that younger people are going to love wearables.

Just looking at the future of Glass illustrates why we think those predictions by others are pathetically low. We would guess that worldwide, Google will sell a minimum of 100 million units of Glass at an average of $300 each over the next three to five years. That's $30 billion alone, and there is a great deal more than that happening in wearables—*a lot more.*

For example, there is an emerging and diverse category of wearable technology called smart textiles,[†††] where contextual capability is literally woven into fabrics. Smart textiles will use sustainable nanotechnology to self-clean, and they will work with other wearable devices as an integrated wearable computer system on the body.

At least a dozen universities, including MIT, Stanford, Yale, the University of Chicago and Carnegie Mellon, are researching wearables. Reports of new and promising wearable technologies are popping up all over the place.

Where is it going? Everywhere. In some cases wearable technologies will even be designed to disappear. At a wearable technology conference in San Francisco in the summer of 2013, sensor-enabled clothing was introduced[†††] that is designed to become transparent when the wearer is sexually aroused.

Genevieve Dion,[†††] an assistant professor and director of the Shima Seiki Haute Technology Lab at Drexel University, told the *Christian Science Monitor* in May 2013 that she dreams of having technology so soft the wearer would not feel anything that changes the feel of the cloth—"No batteries that need to be put into the garment, no small pods that need to go into the pocket," she predicted.

Of course that dream is possible, or soon will be. We live at a time when it's possible to rewire a cockroach brain and strap a little Wifi-enabled back-pack to it so you can control it with your iPhone.[†††] A neural scientist has sanded down the top of a cockroach's head so tiny electrodes can send neural messages to the insect, making it move left or right.

At first, the concept of wearable technology for roaches seemed too bizarre to cover here, but then we started considering the 7 million people in the United States who suffer from such neuralogical disorders as Parkinson's, Alzheimer's, cerebral palsy and multiple sclerosis. Perhaps the "RoboRoaches," as the researchers dubbed them, will lead to cures for serious neurological afflictions.

We selected the following examples to give you some sense that the next generation of devices will go well beyond gizmos that take your pulse or let you check email in a new way:

- **Undergarments that stop assault.** Rape has hit epic proportions in India, where three college students have invented a bra[†††] that gives assailants a shock, and protects the wearer from the jolt with a polymer fabric. The bra automatically alerts authorities via a cell network and a GPS sensor provides precise locations.
- **Cancer-detecting bra**. A Reno company called First Warning Systems, Inc.[†††] offers a "bra system" that provides non-invasive early breast cancer discovery. The bra contains sensors designed to track metabolic patterns at a cellular

level. When an abnormality is detected, the bra system alerts the wearer's physician. The First Warning system started field tests in Summer 2013 after five years of comprehensive research and testing.

- **T-Shirt battery.** A Stanford university team[†††] is working on a T-shirt that will serve as a battery for mobile and wearable devices. It will last for more than 1000 charges. Similar projects have been going on at the Georgia Institute of Technology and in Korea, where Samsung Electronics is said to be working on a "flexible surface prototype."

- **Smart masks**. Many people walking the streets of China's largest cities wear surgical masks as protection from the pervasive air pollution. Sales in Beijing often top 100,000 a day, according to an ABC news report.[†††]

  Now Frog, a global design firm based in San Francisco, has updated the mask into a geomedical device called Frog AirWaves[†††] (not related to Oakley Airwave).

  The mask adds sensors, intelligence and Bluetooth connectivity. Each collects and shares air quality data. A free, government-published mobile app lets users post to a hot map that shows real-time air quality data in the same way that Libelium, the Spanish sensor company, provided radiation-level data in Japan after the Fukushima nuclear disaster.

- **Teenybopper lockets**. The iLocket from Dano[†††] is a $25 little heart-shaped locket that is connected to an Apple iOS mobile app.

  Targeted to young teens, iLocket lets users whisper their most personal secrets into an iPhone or iPad. The app uses speech recognition. Put in a favorite photo of a secret heartthrob and the app prints a photo that fits perfectly inside the locket.

The killer part of the app is how it treats user privacy. Press the locket and the diary entries disappear and remain protected until the iLocket owner unlocks it by pressing the locket again to send a unique code to the iPad app.

Marketers have already started to take contextual technology to the pre-adolescent level. We think there will be many more products aimed at very young consumers who will grow up being increasingly comfortable with technology that might freak their parents out.

The Connected Human

Wearable technology is leading to something we call the "connected human," which describes the intimate and very literal interaction between humans and machines.

We have already reached the point where our technology is becoming an appendage, and we are beginning to integrate with our technologies. They are our assistants, advisors and confidants. They remember what we forget and call for help when we cannot.

Our connected human concept is primarily about people becoming so connected to their devices that to separate them diminishes the capacity of the person. This may sound a bit like Aldous Huxley's *Brave New World*, but in fact it represents a better present world.

This bonding between people and machines will result in people being healthier, better informed, more aware of changes in their environments and more secure, efficient and productive. Today, we usually just carry these devices. Increasingly, we will wear them and ultimately many will physically either attach to or be inserted in us—that is, they will become part of us.

Let's look at the results of the most dramatic cases of physical attachment. In the United States 1.7 million[†††] people have lost limbs. Most of those people have mechanically operated prosthetics. We have been told they can be awkward and frustrating to use.

Jesse Sullivan,[ttt] a former utility lineman from Dayton, Tennessee, lost both arms when a loose wire on a pole jolted him. In 2004, Dr. Todd Kuiken[ttt] of the Rehabilitation Institute of Chicago persuaded Sullivan to become the first to try a pair of experimental prosthetics that were connected to his muscles and nerves. Sullivan now says he can feel his wife's hand when he holds it, and he has experienced the sensation of burning himself when he rested his prosthetic hand too close to a stovetop burner.

Scoble strolled along a cliff overlooking the Pacific Ocean with Chris Tagatac,[ttt] who is paralyzed from the waist down. Tagatac's mobility has been restored thanks to a robotic exoskeleton from Ekso Bionics.[ttt] The device, which fits over Tagatac's clothing, understands weight shifts and thus understands when Tagatac wants to take a step, stand up or sit down.

More of that kind of innovation is coming. We found a handful of U.S. companies making bionic suits that enable paraplegics to walk. Toyota is adapting robots originally developed for their assembly line to serve as at-home personal assistants for physically handicapped people.[ttt]

It's important to understand that, unlike the Borg of science fiction, humans will not become parts of computers, but rather computers will become part of humans. We become the central processors, retaining our hearts, emotions and highly personalized genomics. We still feel the joy of seeing a child's first step, but wearable technology will let us capture and share such moments without failure. We still will feel the agony of a tax audit, but wearables will provide evidence the expense in question was justified.

Although the concept of us as human processing units may sound creepy, it means each of us will have the opportunity to surround ourselves with wondrous new tools that see and hear what we do and, perhaps, can be trusted to remember the moment better.

Among the many wearable products we looked at in researching this chapter was the Plantronics Voyager Legend,[ttt] which is the most contextual Bluetooth headset we have found. It uses sensors to immediately power on the device as soon as you put it on. It knows your environment, so it adjusts noise filters depending on room or wind noise.

When we asked Plantronics CTO Joe Burton,[†††] a savvy industry veteran, just how important he thought wearable technology will be, he told us, "They are bringing about the biggest shift to consumer behavior since the web arrived in 1994."

Devices themselves are, of course, hardware. The real secret to how close and important they are becoming is contained in software, which is becoming the best personal assistant anyone has ever had.

CHAPTER 9

PCAs: Your New Best Friends

Your wish is my command.

Genie to Aladdin

Fiction writers have long fantasized about genies—magical creatures that will do whatever you wish. Over the past 20 years, tech companies have tried to deliver the same sort of magic to users in the form of online assistants. They have consistently failed—sometimes in spectacular fashion.

The idea goes back to the 1980s, when several forgotten hardware companies offered proprietary devices that attempted to manage personal communications, schedules and productivity. Those devices generated much media attention, but mostly they gathered dust on retail shelves. They cost too much and delivered too little.

Then in 1993, Apple CEO John Sculley bet the company and his future on a device called the Newton. The company declared the pioneering hand-held device to be "a complete reinvention of personal computing" creating a new product classification it named "personal digital assistants"—or PDAs.[†††]

The basic Newton cost $699. It introduced the touch screen and hand-writing-recognition software to consumers. The Newton let you manage calendars and contacts by plugging in and synching with your desktop computer. It also enabled users to employ what was then an early version of the internet to send email and text messages.

Apple produced a spectacular launch that was greeted with great fanfare. The media gushed and magazines did cover stories on the dawn of this new PDA age. Competitors rushed alternative devices to market.

But it all fizzled.

The PDA just never took off. It was hard to use and most of those great innovations just weren't ready yet. By 1998, the Newton—and most other PDAs—were either dead or irrelevant. The term itself was quietly erased from the marketing vocabularies of those who had so vigorously embraced it.

Newton today is remembered as Apple's most titanic flop. It makes the more recent Maps gaffe seem like a mere speed bump. The device, named for the man who discovered gravity, almost took Apple down.

Steve Jobs, of course, returned to Apple, and in less than a decade took it from near-death to become the world's most valuable company. Arguably, his defining moment was the introduction of the iPhone in 2007. What people barely noticed was that Newton's core technologies were used in the iPhone, and the device was in fact a greatly refined PDA.

A lot happened between the death of the Newton and the rise of the iPhone: ten more years of Moore's Law making technology more powerful, smaller and less expensive; ten more years of Metcalfe's networks growing exponentially. And don't forget the explosion of the Web and the changes it brought to the lives of people at home and at work, and the blurring of the lines between work and play.

Nearly seven years have passed since the introduction of the iPhone. Social media has changed how people and businesses communicate as the Age of Conversation flowered. We are now mobile much of the time, walking around with data-gathering sensors in our pockets that know where we are, the direction we are heading and whether we are walking, in a car, on a bike or on a skateboard.

By 2013, the term PDA was dead. The revolution incited by the iPhone was won. The promise of omnipresent technology that helps us do what we want to do, like some little genie in our pocket, was achieved.

More Promises to Fulfill

Remember John Malkovich cozying up to Siri by the fireplace in Apple's 2012 ads? Siri was supposed to become our best friend but in reality, she has let us down. She just doesn't work right. All too often she doesn't understand the context of our requests. She gets it wrong far too often.

But other technologies have used less hoopla to come far closer to helping us manage our lives the way a sharp office assistant helps an executive manage her life.

The difference between the PDAs of the '90s and the technologies of today is, of course, context. The new systems understand who you are, what you are doing and what you should know at a particular moment in your ever-changing day. They still make mistakes, but they are getting better as we speak. The new software can discern you and your patterns from other people and their patterns, and it is always on your side.

Once again, baby steps are moving technology forward. One piece of software reminds you when it's your friend's birthday; another sends messages to colleagues when you are stuck in traffic. Soon they'll be talking to the quart of milk in your refrigerator, alerting you when you need to get a fresh carton. These new products keep adding new functionality and they keep improving their ability to understand you.

They learn like curious children: The more time they spend with you, the more they understand you and the smarter they get.

Personal Contextual Assistants

With their roots in the old PDA technology, the new technology goes further. The accent is no longer on being digital, which has become obvious. The accent is on contextual awareness. Rather than PDAs, we call them PCAs— or personal contextual assistants.

PCAs are at the crux of the Age of Context. They will serve many of us better and longer than did the genies of mythology. The time will soon come when not having your own PCA will be like not having email.

PCAs are open, cloud-based mobile platforms. Each is designed to talk with other mobile apps—social media, text, email, Waze traffic and Nooly weather—allowing the PCA to cull connected tidbits and understand how they can impact you at any given moment. Thus, they serve as one-stop spaces to simplify your life, automate redundant and predictable tasks and warn you when a change, such as in the weather, can impact your plans, say, to go sailing or cycling.

They understand how your environment impacts your needs, so they give you different advice depending on whether it's day or night, or a workday or the weekend. They will soon be sufficiently prescient to know if you are in a hurry or have time to stop for a scenic view or a sale at Nordstrom's.

They will understand whether you are headed to work and want to hear only news and traffic reports, or headed home and want to catch up on sports or just kick back and listen to some hip-hop.

Your PCA will evolve into an anticipatory system for nearly every aspect of your life. As the technology gets better and you and your PCA spend more time together, it will understand and anticipate your wishes before you command it—by connecting disparate data dots. These actions will get more sophisticated over time, anticipating more actions and connecting data from multiple sources on an increasingly granular level.

It will alert you when it sees an email conversation that can impact your schedule, perhaps suggesting an action based on your past behavior. In the future, your PCA might see it is unusually hot and suggest remotely telling your lawn sprinkler system to run a few minutes longer.

They work simply enough. Most PCAs send you little reminder notices or "cards" to update you on changes. Some will then ask for permission to take actions on your behalf, such as send a birthday greeting to a friend on Facebook. PCAs are also moving away from keyboard input, which is slower on mobile devices and so dangerous as to be illegal in certain environments, such as when you are driving. They are moving to voice- and gesture-recognition in the near future. Researchers in labs are experimenting with using brainwaves to command inanimate objects, which will make our relationship with our devices even more personal.

Talking with non-human things is not as odd as it sometimes sounds. People already talk with pets and most of us have addressed inanimate objects sharply after tripping over them in the dark. We have become accustomed to telephone voice-processing systems (although we rarely believe our calls are as important to them as they claim).

Array of Choices

Almost all personal PCAs on the market are free services. Each has room for improvement, yet each shows promise in its own way. Their functionality overlaps, but each has an identifiable strong point that might make one better than another for your particular needs.

- Google Now[†††] has the most users and, by virtue of the Google brand, the best market position. It's available on the Android and iOS platforms and is tightly integrated with the ever-expanding Google product suite that includes Search, Gmail, Maps, Talk, Calendar and Drive.

  It is good—some would argue too good—at seeing connections among the data found in diverse apps. Based on what it sees in your online accounts while you are doing other things, it sends you reminder cards about what it thinks you need, "before you even ask," according to marketing material.

  Google is ahead of the pack on the predictive technologies that are the foundation of Google Now. It developed its first predictive search algorithm[†††] back in 2004 for its cornerstone Search product. All this predicting and connecting can be very useful but, as you'll see, it can also go too far.

  What makes Google Now so special is that it has superb voice recognition, the best we've seen in a consumer-level product. As Glass and other wearable products become more prevalent, we think voice input will become extremely important.

- EasilyDo,[†††] available on both iOS and Android platforms, calls itself "your smart assistant" and seems to be just that. Although Google Now focuses primarily on the context of what is happening on Google apps, EasilyDo looks more broadly at your other apps. It notifies you of relevant events and offers to make needed changes for you.

    A big plus is that EasilyDo automates the most mundane tasks, such as updating contacts and calendar appointments. It sees when you get new information and asks your permission to update it for you.

    Additionally, it remembers your login information, making it easy to hop on that scheduled conference call in the car without pulling over to punch in 9687 digits on your phone. It helps you track packages in the same way.

    Mikael Berner, EasilyDo's founder and CEO, says the company intends to perform more tasks than other PCAs, particularly Google Now. As of this writing, EasilyDo was performing 36 tasks, about 25 percent ahead of its leading competitor.

    EasilyDo's newer tasks are becoming more sophisticated: One holds your boarding pass and another calculates your commute time based on real-time traffic conditions. The program will hold your calls during a meeting and find the best data plan during your next overseas trip.

    After less than six months on the market, EasilyDo had about 200,000 daily users, Berner says, and it is partnering with dozens of firms like Evernote, Dropbox, Target and Amazon.

    EasilyDo's current advantage is that it leads as the contextual one-stop service that PCAs aspire to be. By focusing on doing more and more tasks, it seems attuned to what most people will want.

- Atooma[†††] is perhaps the most ambitious of the independent PCAs. It was founded by four Rome-based entrepreneurs and has expanded with offices in Berlin and San Francisco. It has gained notice by winning best-of-show awards at a few EU conferences, including the Italian TechCrunch.

  When we spoke with co-founder Gioia Pistola[†††] in June 2013, she said the year-old start up had built a community of 150,000 regular users, indicating the platform has a chance of reaching critical mass.

  Atooma has many features we like, particularly that it brings in all your essential mobile apps to a single screen you update by simply shaking your phone. Like voice input, gestures such as shaking make it easier and safer to use wearable technology.

  Atooma can be set to automatically turn on Spotify[†††] when you put on your headphones because it knows that's what you usually do. You can also organize work and personal tasks separately and Atooma does an exceptional job of understanding how your context and preferences change between work and play.

  Most of all, we like how Atooma lets users automate their regularly performed tasks in great detail. For example, Atooma can automatically alert family or roommates when you are headed home and switch from 3G to Wifi as you step inside your door.

There are probably another dozen products that fall into this category. Which ones will be the ultimate winners? That won't be clear for a long time. But when competition thrives, users are usually the big winners, because refinements come fast.

It is important to remember that PCAs are platforms. Specific mobile apps, email and social media plug into one or more of them. Some of those apps, however, are starting to blur the lines between platform and stand-alone app. Here's a prime example:

Tempo,††† another innovative offering to come out of SRI, is the most contextual calendar we have seen. It looks deeply into a user's email, calendar, social media and websites, and then brings together relevant emails, addresses, names, phone numbers and more.

Today, Tempo just keeps such related context in your calendar. We assume in the future it will enable automatic warnings to let people know when you are running late and will connect to Waze or maps to alert you when you need to reroute the path to your next appointment.

Creepy Matchmaker

We knew when we started this project that the freaky factor would be a part of our story. We just didn't realize it would play a part in every chapter. We thought PCAs would be the exception but, as we began our research in June 2013, social media pioneer Dave Winer told this story††† on his *Scripting News* blog:

> My friend Jen was coming to visit from [Salt Lake City]. Google Now told me her plane was 24 minutes from arriving at the gate at JFK. I had never told them she was visiting me or what flight she was on (I didn't know). But they did. Probably because she uses Gmail or their calendar, and somehow connected me to that trip (or did they just guess!) and thought I might be impressed if they told me about her flight. I was!
>
> And I felt a little nausea, as I realized they have me by the balls and don't mind if I know it.

If that doesn't make you nervous perhaps the comment Steve Brady, of Australia,††† left on Winer's blog will do the trick:

> I have been getting to know a friend of mine that I met on G+ [Google+] quite well. We live in different cities and have used G+ and Google Talk to stay in touch a lot. Recently she came to visit me and this past weekend I went to visit her.

So imagine my surprise when I go to check my Google Now while at her house and it's giving me directions to a couple of unfamiliar addresses. I showed them to her and she tells me that they are her workplace and the address of friends that she visited recently!

She was a bit freaked out that Google was sharing with me what was essentially private information about her movements. Google has evidently judged that we are close enough that I need to know this information.

You know, it's one thing to declare one's relationship status on social media, it's quite another to have Google decide for me that I'm in a relationship. Because, obviously that's what has happened here. Google has decided that my interactions with Cass are significant enough that we must be in a relationship and has started feeding me information accordingly.

If that's the case, I expect that it will start planning a wedding for us and then one morning I'll wake up to find a calendar entry that it has created, having taken care of booking a venue, catering and inviting guests. The next thing I know Google Now will be suggesting baby names.

In both these cases, a piece of software assumed connections between people before the people involved had decided to make those connections. The PCA shared private information without first getting permission.

This seems to us not only extremely unwise, but also potentially pretty dangerous.

Google needs to remember that people really prefer the right to choose. History is filled with horror stories of incorrectly assumed connections between people that are simply not true, as Americans learned in the McCarthy era back in the 1950s. Currently, we have the U.S. Foreign Intelligence Surveillance Court[†††] (known as the FISA Court for the congressional act that created it). No one is quite certain what it does, but the evidence is growing that it is permitting the National Security Agency to secretly watch U.S. citizens who have the remotest possible connections with suspected terrorists.

Context can fall out of context. For example, after Shel Israel and Robert Scoble published *Naked Conversations,* Israel started seeing Google ads for Victoria's Secret on his Gmail page whenever he mentioned his book. It was funny at the time, but it could have been damaging if the system continued to assume he had a special interest in women's undergarments.

This genie-like magic holds great potential to save time and effort, but these systems need to give users the option to review and correct false assumptions. For Google Now to become that one-stop service on the internet it so clearly aspires to be, it will need to provide users with more control than it did in the cases of Winer and Brady.

Customer-Service PCAs

New technology and good customer service have long been a paradox. Good service improves customer satisfaction, enhances loyalty and strengthens brand—but it can deplete profits. The well-trained, patient technicians required to solve the problems of irate and impatient people are expensive.

The development of the internet has provided large companies with many customer-service alternatives: offshoring, customer forums, FAQs, online automated assistants, untrained and poorly paid humans giving incorrect answers. Israel once had a phone fracas with a United Airlines support person who admitted admit he had never been inside an airport.

Very few customers have much love for any of those options. We don't like being relegated to navigating automated answering decision trees. We don't like waiting for 20 minutes to talk to someone in a call center, where people are trained to find the quickest possible way to get the customer off the phone. We want a sympathetic person who can understand our issues and solve them simply and promptly.

We had come to the point where we had just about given up on this issue. We had resigned ourselves to a lifetime of mediocre service. And then we met Lola.

Lola is attentive, intuitive and accurate. She seems passionate about helping solve our problems, and she is there whenever you need her. Lola is the first customer-service PCA. She is a sophisticated piece of voice interactive software that is being developed at SRI, the lab that gave birth to both Nuance and Siri, for BBVA, a Madrid-based global consumer bank doing business in the EU, the U.S. and Latin America.

When we met Lola in March 2013, she was performing well enough to restore our faith that technology can actually help unhappy customers rather than simply protect companies from them.

Bill Mark,[†††] an SRI VP who leads the Information and Computing Sciences Division, told us the challenge is to get Lola to understand each user's intent and then appropriately act on it by answering questions or actually transferring money from, say, a user's checking account to pay a mortgage loan. A huge factor is that people expect you to remember what they previously said and to understand the nuances and imprecisions of everyday language. This is daunting for computer technology, which is extremely logical and historically not intuitive at all.

Lola can follow conversational shifts as a user goes from checking a balance to making a payment. With uncanny accuracy, she can figure out a user's intent.

"This is really hard. Lola must reason about what to do, and know how to do it in the online banking system. These are difficult challenges," Mark told us.

Dr. Michael Wolverton,[†††] an SRI senior computer scientist, put Lola through a demo where he played the role of a bank customer. He uttered a request in a single, simple sentence and Lola set up an automatic monthly mortgage payment for him. At one point, Wolverton asked Lola about a check for "about $14," and she found four that were close to that amount. In case Lola does screw it up a bit, a real human will monitor conversations and can jump in to help if necessary.

We were impressed with Lola's ability to pick up nuances. At one point, Wolverton intentionally corrected himself. Lola understood and he did not have to start all over again as he would have after a typo on an online bank form.

Because she is software, Lola doesn't suffer such human flaws as distraction, fatigue or mood swings. Her artificial intelligence enables her to get smarter every time she serves a new customer.

We were told that Lola will eventually warn customers if they make a mistake, remind them when their requested action will incur a bank charge and even offer money-saving tips.

Our host, Norman Winarsky, SRI's VP of Ventures, emphasized that SRI owns the foundational technology and sees potential to license it into other industries. So do we.

Lola is named for a real BBVA employee. When the research team interviewed staff, they were impressed with the human Lola's passion and enthusiasm and created the first customer support PCA in her image.

Sometimes, people say they prefer human service to automated agents. Perhaps all we really want is a better quality of service, and to get our problems and requests addressed without delay and frustration. In the past, everyday people were expected to speak a language that computers understood. Lola seems to understand the language we already speak—and she is fluent in both English and Spanish.

Our new PCA best friends are ready to perform some impressive magic on our behalf. The conflict between the magic of contextual technology and the protection of our privacy will be ongoing and will take place in every area of our lives. Perhaps the most important venue for this conflict is where we assume we have the greatest level of privacy: our own homes.

CHAPTER 10

No Place Like The Contextual Home

I long … to be at home wherever I find myself.

Maya Angelou

Dorothy said it first, and it may be a bit overworked, but there really is no place like home. It's a safe haven for you and your loved ones, the most personal of all your spaces. It is where you keep your treasures and your junk.

The contextual age is about to transform a great deal about your home. The Internet of Things will enable inanimate objects to communicate with each other and with you on your mobile device. That device will manage just about everything in your home, and you won't need a keyboard to take up space or slow you down. Having goods and services delivered to your door will be simplified and more efficient.

The result will be safer, sustainable and more secure homes. Hundreds of sensors in the contextual home will connect to you wherever you are. They will literally start at your front door, providing many options for unlocking it. Some mechanisms will be dedicated to just that task; others will be part of larger home-management systems.

Sensor-enabled door locks such as offerings from Lockitron[†††] and Z-wave[†††] fit on your door and respond to commands from a mobile app. Soon they will recognize you and open the door when you arrive, locking it when you leave. They currently sell for as little as $150, and we are sure they will get less expensive. Keyless locks make places safer: Spare keys left under mats or given to house sitters sometimes get into the wrong hands, as police logs demonstrate.

Whether you are around the corner or overseas, you will be able to open your home for authorized people via a mobile app. In an emergency, you can open your door to prevent first responders from battering it down.

Sensor-enabled windows are not new. Adhesive alarm sensors are available at Home Depot for about $30 per window. But they keep getting smaller and cheaper, and now they can be integrated into the pane itself, as they are in car windows. And the new ones can do more than protect you from intruders.

These new windows are contextually aware of interior and exterior environments. They can adjust tinting from transparent to translucent depending on meteorological factors. Some can provide daylight when wanted and convert to mirrors for privacy, eliminating the need for blinds or curtains. They can reduce energy consumption by about 25 percent.[†††]

Smart glass will likely soon contain facial recognition technology as well. When you look at your medicine cabinet mirror in the morning, it will know who you are. While your Bluetooth-enabled toothbrush scans for cavities, you will be able to peruse messages that appear on the glass or see reminders of the medications you need to take.

A whole new smart glass[†††] industry has been incubating for a decade. As the global construction industry comes back to life, the thousands of smart glass installations in North America, Europe, Asia and Australia are evidence of the technology's rapidly escalating adoption rate.

Corning, the world leader in specialized glass and ceramic products, has produced a series of YouTube clips[†††] called *A Day Made of Glass*. In them, every piece of glass in the home contains intelligence and sensors that serve as a ubiquitous contextual computing system. In Corning's vision, the home is one big connected computer and every piece of glass is a screen that you touch to move an image from one glass surface to the next. For example, you can look up a recipe on your phone and drag the result to a space on your stovetop next to your burner as you prepare the dish. If you are video chatting on a smart glass tabletop, you can slide the image onto your TV screen without missing a beat.

Home windows will also serve as huge touch-screen computers or wall-size TVs. In the bedroom, if you hold up a dress on a hanger in front yourself, the smart glass closet mirror will display an image of you wearing it. The mirror can also show you what some of your accessories would add to the outfit.

Corning's concept also goes into the classroom, where all the kids use smart glass computing devices and teachers show wondrous visuals on smart glass boards that contain virtual reality projections, video and 3D animations. The YouTube video takes the kids on a field trip where a ranger creates a life-size *T. rex* snarling among redwood trees.

We wish we believed that such a great classroom vision was imminent, but the reality is that most classrooms lag far behind the technology that many children use today at home. In fact, you could argue some children are learning more online than in class.

One piece of Corning's vision seems to be pretty close to reality though. Samsung has introduced a table whose entire surface is a touch-screen computer;[†††] it sells for a mere $8400. And Corning is reportedly developing a 46-inch touch-screen wall display that will let you toggle between computer, game console and HDTV. When not in use, the device will serve as a transparent window.

Household PCAs

Many available products are designed to make your home more contextual and make remote management easier. We call them household PCAs because they are an obvious subset of the personal contextual assistants we introduced in Chapter 9.

Among the most impressive is SmartThings,[†††] a cloud-based platform that uses a mobile app and sensors to let you manage a home's locks, lights, temperature and power. The system notifies you when it sees changes and alerts you if it perceives a problem.

SmartThings sprang from very practical roots. Founder Alex Hawkinson[†††] says he developed the platform after he and his wife arrived at their Colorado home late one night to discover that cold weather had ruptured a water pipe.

The system is smart enough to understand your current activity. For example, if it sees you have gone to bed, SmartThings makes sure your doors are locked and the lights are off. It is an open platform—the company hopes growth will come from adding not only its own apps, but new functionality from third-party sources.

Austin-based WigWag,[†††] a similar household PCA, is even younger than SmartThings. When we talked with founder-CEO Ed Hemphill in July 2013, he was raising funds on Kickstarter,[†††] the popular crowd-funding site.

WigWag is also an open platform that performs tasks similar to those done by SmartThings. What differentiates WigWag are the sensor packs that you set up in each room. The sensors detect unexpected changes, such as patio motion or garden frost, and alert you via text message. They also tell your mobile app when to remotely adjust lights and appliances.

Hemphill argues that WigWag has the edge in ease of use: Any family member (even children) or weekend guests can use WigWag without special instruction, he asserted.

CubeSensors[†††] works a little differently. Composed of battery-powered, two-square-inch sensor-laden cubes, CubeSensors is more of an environmental PCA watchdog. The cubes measure noise, pollution, lights and humidity—invisible elements that can cause discomfort or worse. The sensors transmit data to a cloud-based app that analyzes and recommends adjustments or sends danger alerts, such as for carbon monoxide pollution.

Carbon monoxide emissions injure about 20,000 people annually in the United States and kills about 500. CubeSensors are designed to prevent such tragedies.

Contextual TV

Our homes may be growing smarter, but the activity that takes up many of our waking hours seems to be dumbing down. The average American spends almost 160 hours a month watching traditional TV[†††]—most of it crap.

But as computers and TVs converge, a screen will be just a screen and we will watch whatever we want, regardless of the source.

One touch of irony is that as the PC has become smaller, simpler and less expensive over the years, the TV has grown larger, more complex and expensive. We bet there are more wires and plugs behind your TV than at your computer workstation—if you still have a computer workstation. We bet you can navigate online with greater ease than on your TV channel guide.

It is frustrating for most people to find content they like among the hundreds of channels offering thousands of programs. We must sift through a great deal of crap before we can find something that is a gem for us. So mostly, we stick with watching the same shows.

But as context comes to the remote, or the devices replacing it, we have found an almost-overwhelming array of apps to help you home in on your desired content. Three we like:

- NextGuide[†††] is an iPad app used by millions of people. It learns what each user in the house likes and personalizes the programs it offers accordingly. It may notice that you like Brad Pitt movies. So, even though it sees you don't watch talk shows, it tells you when Pitt is going to be a guest on *Letterman*. It also lets you automatically share what you like with selected Facebook friends.

  You can also go private, so no one knows you have a secret penchant for *Army Wives*. In this age of eroding privacy, we feel strongly that there should be more places like NextGuide where we have the right to opt out of sharing. We discuss the issue of privacy in greater depth in Chapter 12.

- **Comcast,** the world's largest cable carrier, is rolling out its next-generation X1 platform,[†††] which enables voice control of cable entertainment content over mobile phones. It is migrating set-top box functionality to the cloud. This enables downloads to arrive twice as fast, and for the system to store user preference data. The new voice-recognition search enables you to speak the name of an actor, team, or title and get contextually appropriate results.

- **Vidora** is an iPad app that eliminates the need for a set-top box altogether. We found it easy to locate content we like—which seems to be the whole point. Vidora also studies what you watch to suggest new content you might like.

User-Friendly Gestures

Movea[†††] is a leader in gesture-enabling technology that is used mostly in sports and fitness devices. It has also begun to provide technology for internal mapping on smartphones. To do that it needs to understand, not just where you are going, but also whether you are on an escalator or if those metal things in front of you are train tracks. It is also providing TV owners with an entirely new way to operate their systems.

As an OEM company, Movea licenses its MoveaTV technologies to be used in Samsung, Philips and other major brand HDTV remotes to let you navigate your TV set the way you might work a Wii or Nintendo game console. It also is a component in the new Comcast X1 set-top boxes.

Dave Rothenberg,[†††] Movea director of marketing and partner alliances, argues that gestures are easier, faster and more natural for navigating. And because Movea is part of other devices, you can play gesture-enabled games on your TV, saving about $300 on the cost of a game console.

Tens of millions of home systems already use Movea gesture control, according to Rothenberg. Orange,[†††] the French communications giant, had shipped 100 million of them by mid-2013.

Rothenberg argues that users who try gesture controls often prefer them to other options. He referred to a recent Philips study of 200 Danish homes, where gesture-enabled controls resulted in a dramatic increase in paid subscriptions to premium content—the ultimate goal of content providers.

The contextual piece is that Movea learns the nuances of your gestures and adapts to them, over time decreasing the time it takes to find what you want. It also learns which family member is using the remote.

Tapping in to the Internet of Things, Rothenberg says that Movea wants to connect your remote to other household objects. For example, MoveaTV might time your microwave popcorn to coincide with a commercial break.

Movea also offers MoveaMobile, which enables you to navigate computing devices or operate household appliances using gestures to turn on lights, a faucet or a dishwasher.

Movea is not the only company focused on the growing area of gestures. As we move into the Age of Context, keyboards make less sense than voice and gesture input.

Anther promising gesture innovator is Leap Motion,[†††] which makes a cute little activating touchpad that enables you to do all sorts of things by gesture on your desktop computer, including art, graphics, games, hand-writing, drawing, map navigation, photo blowups and more.

Gesture technology has been around for a long time. It dates back to the 1980s when Nintendo introduced the awkward and ill-fated Power Glove.[†††] Currently, the most advanced gesture technology is Microsoft Xbox One with Kinect, a $500 platform that now includes sensors good enough to determine a player's excitement level by measuring heartbeats.[†††]

Microsoft unofficially confirms it sees a future in the home for Kinect that goes beyond its use in Xbox game platforms. Microsoft recently added a Skype version to its voice-command-operated Xbox. We can see the day when Kinect joins the fray as a gesture-enabled PCA. Perhaps someday it will connect to your family robot.

Microsoft has churned out a few interesting additional consumer apps in recent times, not the least of which is Blink,[†††] a unique Windows feature that lets you hold down your camera shutter to grab quick blink-like bursts of brief video clips. You choose what you like and the clip expands and can be shared with friends in true social media fashion.

We were also impressed with MYO, from Thalmic Labs, a startup based in Ontario. It is a band that you strap onto your forearm that reads electrical muscle activity, enabling users to control a broad range of activities on a desktop or mobile computer.

A YouTube video[†††] shows someone using MYO to play iTunes music with a finger snap, navigate an online ski run and play all sorts of games. It shows a child move a ball with gestures and an adult make an object hover and move in mid-air. Most intriguing was a military person navigating a miniature driverless car with gestures.

As we wrote this in July 2013, MYO had not yet shipped, but it had taken pre-orders that backed up into 2014.

1-Click Delivery

We never thought that our search for elements of the modern contextual home would lead us to a contextual refrigerator magnet from a pizza joint in Dubai. But that is precisely what we discovered in Red Tomato Pizza.[†††]

The key component is the Red Tomato VIP Fridge Magnet, which is exactly what it sounds like. It's a little plastic pizza box that you stick to your refrigerator. When you flip it open and press the button, you've automatically ordered your favorite pizza. A text message confirms your order and estimates the delivery time.

We are not suggesting that you order your pizza from Dubai when you live in Des Moines, but we do predict that such 1-click ordering will be very much a part of life in the contextual home.

This is one of several examples of a trend we love: the Uberization of business services. Like the Uber cars, Red Tomato Pizza comes to you. These businesses use stored data to personalize the business transaction but make it easy for customers to change their mind. They use mobile apps so customers can track delivery progress and simplify payments by having a credit card on record.

They are not alone. Other services like eBay Now and Amazon Local are coming close. Soon the smartest operators of supermarkets, dry cleaners and other merchants will Uberize their services as well.

Connecting All the Things

We've talked about the Internet of Things. We believe that a part of it will be households of connected things. Anything in your home that has an on-off switch will be interconnected. All glass objects will be connected as well. Ubiquitous sensors will be a part of it as well, as, of course, will your front door.

All of these things will communicate with you wherever you are, through some form of PCA. They will also connect to emergency services, utilities and the entire Internet of Things.

Everywhere we looked we found companies that were building little pieces of the new contextual household. Belkin and Philips, for example, are working on getting their many home products to talk with each other and with all your other fixtures and devices.[†††]

One of the earliest connected device is the Nest Thermostat, which remembers what temperatures you like and turns itself down when you leave the room, often resulting in significant utility bill savings. PintoFeed enables you to feed your pet remotely and check to see if Tabby or Rover is healthy and eating right.[†††]

A contextual infrastructure is being built to accommodate all these mundane but useful connected objects. For example, Belkin's Conserve Surge Protector[†††] is a $30 device that looks like the any other surge protector you can buy in a supermarket. But it comes with a remote switch that lets you simultaneously shut down six plugged-in devices, eliminating the "phantom power" that often represents about 10 percent of your monthly electric bills.

Tom Raftery,[†††] who writes GreenMonk,[†††] our favorite environmental blog, told us about the Belkin WeMo (short for "We Movement"), which connects outlets, motion sensors, baby monitors and webcams by Wifi. With WeMo's mobile app you can switch your appliances on or off, listen in on your baby and even check a webcam from anywhere to ensure an elderly relative is okay.

Raftery also pointed us to Belkin's Echo[†††] Water, Electricity and Natural Gas sensor devices, due to come out in 2014 and 2015. They will be inconspicuous little attachments to home systems, allowing homeowners to analyze and report on usage.

The Eco Sensor Water-Saving Tap[+++] (not to be confused with the Belkin Echo brand) works like many faucets in public restrooms. It is targeted to parents whose children forget to turn water off, as well as people who have arthritis or cognitive issues such as Alzheimer's.

Philips is developing disposable sensors that can detect spoilage in your refrigerator, or when it's time to clean carpets, towels or clothing.

GE's Grid IQ[+++] is an "insight tool" that mines social media for geo-tagged mentions of electrical outages, allowing utility companies to respond faster. Data is fed to hot maps where patterns alert crews and first responders to power outages, floods, tornadoes or fires.

Could such smart grids prevent such tragedies as the one caused by the massive forest fire that took the lives of 19 Arizona firefighters in June 2013? Perhaps not quite yet. But they are coming closer all the time.

Robotic Household Assistants

Another category of personal assistants for the home steps out of the pages of science fiction and perhaps meanders over the freaky line.

Robots have long existed as characters in books and movies. More recently they have started taking over the most tedious jobs in automated factories and some of the most dangerous first-response work, such as disarming explosive devices. Now robots are finding roles in the home. In some cases they are serving as novelty possessions for the affluent in Asia.

In India, robot maids are used by some of the country's uppercrust. The Times of India,[+++] a favorite publication of the nation's elite, alleged that it was because robots are less prone to tantrums than the humans they are replacing. We suspect that it's also because they don't mind the tantrums of their employers.

In Japan, researchers are developing a household robot called AR, for Assistant Robot.[+++] With processing power and sensors sophisticated enough to see objects in 3D, it can perform such complex chores such as ironing and dishwashing.

Our relationship with our devices is going to emerge into something new and different in the coming Age of Context. Talking with our mobile devices is one level, but being greeted at the door by the family robot, that takes your coat and fetches your slippers, will bring a whole new dimension of service into our lives.

There has never been a place like the contextual home. Our faucets and our thermostats will be sending us messages. Our mobile apps will be sending suggestions to our smart mirrors. But these will be useful messages, messages sent by devices that understand what we need to know.

It will be a direct and welcome contrast to the ubiquitous marketing messages we get every day that very often have nothing to do with our information needs, location or activity.

We refer of course to the direct marketing and advertising industries.

CHAPTER 11

Pinpoint Marketing

In the world of advertising, there's no such thing as a lie. There's only the expedient exaggeration.

Roger Thornhill, *North by Northwest*

Sometimes marketing is like magic. It can capture your dreams and take you to imaginary places. Usually, it is more like the sound of a cat fight—intruding on your peace and leaving you frazzled. Marketing and advertising deliver far more noise than signal. Most of us, it seems, would just like it to go away. But despite the mute and fast-forward functions on our TVs and software filters, the crap just keeps on coming.

Marketing was once about companies building relationships with customers and prospects; branding was about building emotional attachments. Now it seems it's mostly about money—lots and lots of money. We don't fault companies for wanting to make money. We even do a little marketing ourselves to boost book sales.

If there were a way to make marketing more relevant to our needs, we would embrace the companies that send the messages. We might even voluntarily become user champions, spreading word-of-mouth praise for the company and its products.

We believe such changes will happen in the coming Age of Context, when the smartest and most forward-thinking companies will send messages to their customers using the five forces. The result will be lower marketing costs and dramatically higher response rates.

Context will allow us to receive messages based on location, time of day, season and what we intend to do next. We believe this will dramatically boost response rates because customized messages will be more relevant to the recipients. An ad for a discount at a nearby restaurant when we are hungry is pretty likely to get us to act immediately.

Unfortunately, we cannot promise an immediate death of the stuff that sounds like a cat fight. We think those annoyances will taper off slowly over the next decade or so. We can't wait. We will miss the noise of those untargeted messages as much as the colonoscopies that sensor-embedded pills will replace.

As users we will have far greater control over who can send us messages. We will be able to filter out the ones we do not want, by topic, source or mood-of-the-moment.

The 2 Percent Intrusion

If most people hate most marketing most of the time, why are we all inundated with these ads? Shel Israel learned the answer back in 1995 when he worked for a large PR agency, and MCI, a now-defunct telecom company, was his client. The company pushed its discount phone service by having call center employees phone people at home at dinnertime.

Israel told his client that every time he mentioned MCI in conversations, people became irate, because they hated those intrusive calls. The client confided he, too, had the same experience. Sometimes it got so bad that he avoided disclosing who he worked for.

Israel asked him why he didn't drop the campaign. The client stared at him in disbelief. "Are you crazy?" he asked. "We pull in a 2 percent national favorable response. It grabs a 3 percent response in rural areas and urban minority areas."

"What about the 98 percent of the people who hate you for calling," Israel asked.

"Screw 'em," he replied. "We're getting rich off the 2 percent."

Therein lies a statistical paradox: At least 98 percent of all advertising or marketing messages are ignored or detested, but a response rate of just 0.5 percent makes such efforts worthwhile, and above a 2 percent response makes direct response campaigns profitable, often extremely so.[†††]

So when someone sends out 10 million emails, as is so often the case, they don't really care that 9,800,000 people ignored or were annoyed by the intrusion.

Direct marketers prefer getting that 2 percent on the internet rather than on radio or television because the costs are lower. In fact, the cost of direct online campaigns is so low that an unsavory marketer can send out 10 million emails for only $500. For a mere $69, she can buy a software bot from another online direct marketer that puts out tens of thousands of email messages in just a few seconds.[†††] Response rates may be low for such crude efforts, but they are high enough for marketers to keep sending them.

Thus we get treated to all those offers to lose ten pounds in ten days, or prosper by buying up foreclosed homes, or earn a multimillion-dollar commission by helping some Ethiopian heir launder money through our bank accounts. "It's that easy," the marketer promises, and it is that easy—for them.

Most people relegate such tripe to the spam bucket. Google has begun to fight spam with contextual filters. But as such tools emerged on email, the bad guys found new points of attack, such as Facebook, Twitter, LinkedIn, Foursquare and other social networks.

It's a Cold War. The better our tools to evade direct marketing messages become, the more new ways the marketers will find to intrude on our space.

False Context

You've probably heard of "contextual advertising." It started when Google introduced the AdSense network in 2003. When Google's web crawler began to scan tens of millions of pages of content, matching ads to content by targeting keywords, contextual advertising was born.[†††]

If you search for flights to Maui, for example, you might receive an ad for a nice deal on a place to stay. However, if after you returned you were looking up the name of the wonderful little shop you discovered up-island, you might see the same offer. In the former situation the ad is relevant; in the latter it's worthless.

Sometimes such ads are beneath worthless; they are downright tasteless. When tech author and journalist Steven Levy[†††] tweeted that a plane had crashed at San Francisco International Airport in June 2013, he reported that an Expedia ad suddenly appeared "urging me to fly somewhere on vacation." Such gaffes are far from uncommon and often leave a long-lasting negative impression on the very people they are trying to attract.

Sometimes ads jump in at the right time—but they just don't know when to quit. When Israel blogged that he wanted advice on buying a new refrigerator, friends mentioned KitchenAid as a good choice, and he almost immediately saw an ad for a closeout model at a great price. Five years later, the web pages he visited were still being peppered with ads for refrigerators, dishwashers, toaster ovens and sundry kitchen appliances before they finally trickled to a halt.

In short, we disagree with Google's claim that their ads are contextual. Their advertising system does not have an awareness of our personal patterns. It has no sense of time; it does not understand what we are doing or where we are doing it when it puts content in front of us.

The ad system cannot tell if we are hungry or cold, thirsty or lonely. It does not know our intent. Marketing messages would be a lot better received if they could be targeted not to our eyeballs as they are today, but to our intentions and our immediate environments as they increasingly will be in the Age of Context.

The Intention Economy

Doc Searls,[†††] co-author of the groundbreaking *Cluetrain Manifesto*, wrote a new book in 2012, *The Intention Economy—When Customers Take Charge*. That book proposes to wrest marketplace controls from sellers and give them to buyers.

When you want to go to Italy, you would go to an internet space and declare your intention. You would get offers from airlines, hotels, restaurants, museums and places to visit. Once you declare your choices, all marketing bids would stop.

 As Searls describes it, the mechanism has many moving parts, but we think if it were applied and refined over time, the idea has merit.

A few companies already create online marketplaces where the buyer is in control. Priceline.com lets you post where you want to go and how much you are willing to pay, and vendors compete for your travel dollars. CrowdSPRING has created a similar graphic design marketplace.[†††]

Searls, we think, may go too far in trying to give all the controls to the buyers—a marketplace needs some give-and-take to operate optimally. And today's sellers would benefit from employing less- objectionable methods when they approach buyers.

We expect the Intention Economy to be a significant factor in how marketplaces will evolve in the new Contextual Age—and we expect that evolution to be rapid. A second factor will be the ability for sellers to hyper-personalize their offerings to each customer.

One-to-One

For a few years in the 1950s, Israel's father, Barney Israel, was a door-to-door salesman, a common profession during simpler times. He knocked on strangers' doors, showing them samples of what he had to sell.

Sometimes a prospect wasn't interested in what he offered but voiced a desire for an item he didn't carry. The senior Israel would search around and find the item, returning later to sell it for a small markup. He wasn't interested in the profit so much as making his customer loyal to him.

This is one-to-one marketing in its simplest form. The way Barney Israel practiced it was not very efficient and could not scale, but it demonstrated the essential premise: Understand what the customer wants and fulfill the need before someone else does. Another way of looking at it: Bring your business to the customer rather than make your customer come to you.

Bringing It Online

In 1993 Don Peppers and Martha Rogers published *The One-on-One Future,* which made the case for shifting marketing focus from product to customer. It pioneered the idea of personalization in marketing.

That revolutionary approach to marketing evolved into customer relationship management (CRM), a powerful method for building brand loyalty. When it formed in 1999, salesforce.com[†††] based its CRM services entirely in the cloud and made that the differentiating factor against competitors. It was wildly successful.

As social media developed, Salesforce leveraged it to more efficiently market to customers by actually engaging them in conversations. This shift from "message mongering," as we called it in *Naked Conversations,* to interactive conversations is called "social CRM," a phenomenon that has moved the enterprise closer to true contextual marketing. Social CRM enables companies and customers to collaborate on products, support policy and other issues.

Social CRM and online communities have done much to improve understanding and trust between companies and customers. Most companies that use it assign an employee to help customers find what they want through their online communities. Successful customer relationship managers never message monger on their employer's behalf. The company's customers, analysts, media, investors and future employees become a wise crowd, helping each other. They do it faster and often with passion, while the company saves on resources.

Social CRM is Barney Israel's style of one-to-one marketing—on steroids. It enables global companies to use the internet to scale personalization by orders of magnitude. These online communities create the sort of marketplace that Searls envisioned in at least one critical way: The customers have to go somewhere and state what they want.

Our vision encompasses that, but we think that marketing in the Age of Context can be so efficient that buyers won't need to go anywhere special, or declare their intentions. Sellers will be able to come to them when mobile, social media, sensors, data and location technologies indicate that the customers are in the mood for a particular product or service.

We call it "Pinpoint Marketing."

Zeroing In

Pinpoint Marketing is the ability of sellers to offer goods and services in the context of where you are and what you are doing, and to anticipate what you want to do next. Sellers can compete for your business by being more accurate in their predictions. And marketers will know when to stop trying as your context changes.

We've already given you examples of Pinpoint Marketing. Remember the contextual beers at Gillette Stadium? The Patriots use mobile technology to give customers what they want, when they want it, and they do it more easily than had been possible before.

The Patriots know the patterns of their best customers and anticipate what they might want next. They don't compete with the game by broadcasting messages to all 70,000 fans, but they do pinpoint a relatively small number of prime fans and are likely to get a very high response. And the offers to selected fans remain invisible to anyone who could not take advantage of the deal anyway.

Pinpoint Marketing strategies reverse the traditional tenets of mass marketing. Instead of spending more money to reach more people, Pinpoint Marketing enables sellers to spend less money to reach fewer people but achieve a much higher response rate.

The Patriots program has just started and they did not reveal to us much about their long-term strategy, but we have our own ideas about it. For example, we see a huge opportunity to upsell other stadium fans.

The Patriots will gather data on the patterns of their best customers this year. They are learning what they order and when. Many customers will order the same food at the same time.

Let's suppose it's a cheesesteak and beer, ordered by the phone app 15 minutes before the half, picked up in the express line three minutes into the break. But one week, the Patriots send 50 to 100 of those select fans a special offer one hour before the break: a 40 percent discount on a Pinot and a steak at a reserved table in the clubhouse.

As the invited fans arrive in the dining area, the staff recognizes them by their online photo, addresses them by name and ushers them to a nice table where the Pinot is waiting and their hot and sizzling steaks are delivered just a moment later.

As the lucky fans depart, their tables are made ready for another 50 to 100 fans who have received similar offers for a clubhouse repast at a slightly later time slot. Maybe, half become regular clubhouse patrons. The same goes on at other NFL stadiums, and over time that makes a nice little incremental revenue boost.

But wait, there's more, as the guy on the late-night infomercial used to say. On that same first Sunday, someone in the long beer line for regular fans looks with envy at the express line and expresses envy on Facebook. A few minutes later, the Pats send that fan a message offering him a free pass and a discount to the express line the next time he's at Gillette Stadium.

Now the Patriots have started a supply chain of upgrading fans. They increase loyalty and revenue. Because they do it so efficiently, the only cost to them is a discount on the newly anointed prime fan's first meal or beverage.

As we mentioned in Chapter 3 on retailing, such services are likely to spread to pro basketball, baseball, soccer, hockey and wrestling venues, as well as to concert halls, theaters and racetracks. In a while, such programs will find their way to university-level events. There's really no stopping such programs once they take off.

Compare the marketing impact and effectiveness of such programs to a TV spot depicting a paunchy retired player inviting people to try the Gillette Clubhouse dining room at the next game, or a cutout coupon in the Boston Phoenix. Which would be most likely to make you a customer? Which will make you more loyal to the organization?

Pinpoint will not kill mass marketing, but it will cause a little bruising that will never heal. Slowly, over time, the new approach will grow and the old one will shrink. At first, traditional marketers will disdain Pinpoint as being only able to bring in pocket change. Then they will become angry as Pinpoint distracts customers and siphons away revenue. Then the traditional marketers will try to adapt, but by then it will be too late.

The New One-to-One

Many consumer-focused organizations separate their IT operations in functional silos, and that creates significant barriers to successful Pinpoint Marketing. Four separate internal IT systems—dining, front desk, golf/activities and meetings—at Robert Scoble's beloved Ritz-Carlton don't talk to each other. If you make dinner reservations, the restaurant doesn't need to make you a special offer because you already intend to show up. If you are a regular, the maître d' may offer you your favorite beverage as you are seated or bring you that chocolate soufflé that you reviewed so favorably on Yelp after your last visit.

But if the four silos were open and connected, sharing their data, then the rest of the Ritz could offer you additional services. The spa and golf courses could entice you to come a bit earlier. The reservation desks could offer you a free post-golf changing room so you could see how great those rooms are. Then they could tempt you to spend the night at half-price in a room the Ritz knows will go unfilled anyway. If, from your room, you see a little speck in the ocean from your window that could be a whale, the Ritz might offer you a special deal with the local whale-watching excursion boat and, for the outing, perhaps a discounted windbreaker from one of their shops.

The hotel could personalize your visit in so many ways. What starts with dinner reservations could be converted into a memorable time, one that you may want to repeat and share with friends. But IT systems have to talk to each other before this scenario will be possible, and the hotel will need to leapfrog into the Age of Context by using mobile, social media, data, sensors and location technologies to know their customers and prospects well enough to personalize services and offers.

What would motivate the Ritz to embark on a Pinpoint Marketing campaign such as this? They already have a highly regarded brand and have survived recent economic tough times unscathed. Our guess is they will be moved to change because a challenger will need to try such a new approach to compete with an entrenched market leader. The Ritz will then have to follow suit or give a trailing competitor a chance to pull ahead.

Eliminating Sneaky

For many years online marketers have used a sly little piece of software known as a "cookie" to spy on you. When you register on a site, the vendor slips a cookie into your computer, where it collects data on you and reports back to the vendor when you return to the site.

Cookies are not all bad. They let the vendor's site greet you by your name and remember your buying history. The vendor knows how often you visit and what may have previously caused you to leave the site without purchasing anything.

Many users don't mind that level of personalization. What they do mind is that cookies feel sneaky. Most sites don't ask you before inserting a cookie on your computer. Frequently, the site's rarely read Terms of Use or Privacy Policy mention that by using the site you are granting it the right to put a cookie on your machine. We guess that's because many users would say no if asked directly.

Personally, we prefer vendors that show they respect the user's right to choose. Contextual technologies don't use cookies. Most smartphone apps ask your permission to push messages at you and to know your location. True, many users don't yet understand the implications of these requests, but at least there is some attempt to get permission before marketing to you.

Users also have the right to turn off Notifications whenever they wish, and doing so is a relatively simple task. If you opt out, you will be left alone, but if you opt in, you may find the messages you receive to be increasingly worthwhile.

Glass Ad Empty

So far, we've mostly focused on marketing via phones and tablets, where, after a couple of years of trial and error, companies like Facebook seem to be finally figuring out how to make mobile ads work.[†††]

Just as advertisers are catching up on the last generation of devices such as phones and tablets, a new generation is coming in the form of wearable devices such as Google Glass, the Pebble smart watch and even computerized socks.[†††]

These spell trouble for advertisers because the new devices either have tiny screens or no screens at all.

As of this writing, Google has placed temporary advertising bans on Google+, Google Now and Google Glass. But the world's largest online ad platform is going to have to make money in the Age of Context somehow.

We think a new form of Pinpoint Marketing is the answer. We also think it will be popular with users and even more lucrative for Google than ads have been.

The solution we envision will be in the form of micro commissions. Google Glass will know not only where you are but whether you are driving, on foot or riding a bicycle. Understanding the context of your activity, location, the time of day and weather would greatly influence what you might want to do or buy next.

Let's walk through an example:

It's noon on a hot day in July a few years hence. Glass sees you have been on a long bike ride and now you are resting in the shade of a tree. You ask Glass to tell you where you can get a drink (not currently a command), and it tells you there is a mall a quarter of a mile away. It suggests an organic shop that has iced fruit drinks. When you enter the establishment, Google receives a small percentage of the price of what you purchase. Google earns a commission for delivering a customer.

Now let's return to that tree by the road. It's mid-winter and the temperature is slightly north of zero. A snowmobiler puts his vehicle on idle and asks Glass where to get a drink. This time Glass offers up a place in the same mall that serves hot chocolate, and another offering beer and Irish coffee. The intrepid snowmobiler makes a selection. Google gets a tiny commission.

This makes marketing informational and very useful. No ads are needed and stores are happy to pay a little bit for a real customer.

Perhaps Google will get paid just for getting the cyclist and the snowmobiler to just take a look. It has an old patent for technology that would enable a "pay per gaze" system, which would of course make Google happier than the stores—if Google opts to use that method. In either case, the user does not have to be bombarded with unwanted offers to visit the manicure salon in the same mall.[†††]

This same micro commission system could work on other devices. In the future, a Fitbit could detect from your blood sugar that you are hungry. It could talk to a mobile device that knows the time of day, your location and your food preferences. Without you doing anything, the mobile device suggests a few nearby places to eat. You pick one and the vendors of both devices share a tiny commission.

Such payments may be small, but eventually there could be billions of them every day. When that happens, advertisers and marketers that use massive message distribution to garner a microscopic percentage of advertising will provide too little value and will slowly vanish from marketing mix strategies.

Google is not alone. One of its traditional rivals may be embarking on a similar micro-commission strategy, or at least it looks that way to us.

Micro Sales by Satori

In Buddhism, satori, or enlightenment, is the first step on the path toward nirvana. It is also likely to be a big step toward the re-emergence of Microsoft as a pre-eminent force in consumer technology.

Microsoft Satori is the result of many years of quiet internal rethinking at the Redmond giant. Its aim is to help users of its devices and services find the right paint color for a room, for example, or understand the migration patterns of whales from the beach where they are watching them.

Satori takes Bing's ability to crawl 10 trillion internet sites and integrates it with data from such significant partners as Facebook, LinkedIn, Twitter and Foursquare to build a digital copy of the physical world; it will become a contextual engine driving all Microsoft and partner applications.

Satori is an extremely ambitious project. Employing a massive amount of machine learning, it is trying to re-create the entire physical world, everything in it, and the relationships among all those things.

So, as you talk to a friend on a social network and mention you should get together for dinner, a user-authorized, Satori-powered system could find a night that's open to you both and suggest restaurants that you both like in convenient locations that won't be hard to reach based on traffic predictions for that night.

Once you select an option, Satori would serve up competitive offers from nearby restaurants that might attempt to hijack your business.

Although Microsoft did not mention micro commissions when we talked with them, this seems a very logical step toward a new form of revenue, and as good a value proposition for Satori as it is for Glass.

Perhaps Microsoft plans to have a Glass of its own. The company recently reorganized into a "devices and services company." We find it interesting that software seems relegated to a lesser role.

The new organization makes Microsoft structure more like that of its archrivals Google and Apple. Microsoft is clearly the underdog in the current landscape, but Stefan Weitz argues that through its alliances and its own significant data stockpile, Microsoft will understand more about real-world people, places and things than any other company, and Satori will be the most contextual data engine available.

Will Satori overcome the significant leads of its rivals? That remains to be seen. But we believe that users will benefit by having another significant player in the game, and the one that offers end users the best and most relevant deals the most often may be the ultimate winner in what promises to be a lengthy battle.

Diverted Customers

"Plus one-minus one" is a sales and marketing term that refers to when you gain a customer that your competitor loses. VinTank, the California wine country startup that geo-fences wineries and other leisure destinations is an example of how context lets you implement plus one-minus one. When one winery's premium customer drives past a competitor's tasting room, a well-timed offer can hijack that buyer, just as Satori might do with competitive offers.

The same technology and tactics can be used in many ways. For example, if you intend to buy shoes at Nordstrom's, Bloomingdale's sees your intent and may offer you a better deal on those red pumps you crave.

Tagwhat[†††] is a mobile app that lets vendors compete for your business as you walk, jog or drive along, giving you messages relevant to your activity, your location and the time of day. What we like best is Tagwhat's noise-abating filtering system. It lets you control what you see based on your mood or intent.

If you are strolling in a mall, you can see what special offers are waiting for you inside each shop. But if you prefer a little nightlife in nearby clubs, you can filter out retail offers and display messages about which bands are playing and at what time. Like other contextual apps, Tagwhat will learn your taste over time.

Those filters matter. Without them, it would be like walking through Times Square on a busy night with messages coming at you from every direction. You would probably be overwhelmed and retreat to a less message-infested neighborhood.

By tapping into Facebook and other social networking platforms, Tagwhat lets you see—or perhaps hear—what people you trust have to say, helping you make decisions.

Tagwhat is a young company. It may be acquired before it has to decide how to monetize. But if it has to choose, we think that advertising would ruin the product, just like we think it would hurt Glass.

We see the future for both companies in micro commissions. We see micro commissions as a monetization system that could disrupt or destroy the most banal forms of marketing, and we believe both buyers and sellers will benefit from their demise.

Dark Sides

We'd love to be able to predict that contextual technology will usher in an era of such wonderment that unwanted messages will disappear and that all apps will be designed to increase user options. Unfortunately, not all contextual marketing will be designed with your desires in mind.

ThinkNear, recently acquired by Telenav, a turn-by-turn direction vendor, allows businesses to shoot ads at you when you get within 100 meters of them. Filters are not included.†††

Scoble visited PARC, Silicon Valley's oldest research center, for a full day in August 2013 and saw several promising technologies. One area is called contextual intelligence. We saw similar technology earlier at SRI, where researchers are using it to determine if troubled war veterans may be contemplating suicide by using contextual technology to determine mood.†††

PARC's research team is working on using their version for more business-oriented purposes. The system would use phone sensors to determine your mood, and then feed that information to marketers and employers.†††

PARC's focus is technology, not application, but as we thought about contextual intelligence, we worried about how this new technology could be used without user permission or knowledge.

Could an employer track an employee, after giving her a bad review, to see if this darkened the employee's mood or caused depression? Can marketers make offers to you based on how you feel, even when you have no intention of sharing such information?

Frankly, we don't see how this can be prevented. Such mood detection would follow a marketing tradition established back in the 1950s and documented by Vance Packard's *The Hidden Persuaders*. Packard wrote about how advertisers learned that the best way to sell a young man a red convertible was to show one with an attractive woman in the passenger seat.

Throughout this book, we've referred to the balance between the benefits and dark sides of the Age of Context. Perhaps the most complex, controversial and sometimes volatile dark side is the issue of user privacy.

CHAPTER 12

Why Trust Is The New Currency

You have zero privacy anyway. Get over it.

Scott McNealy, co-founder, Sun Microsystems

U p to this point, we have extolled the virtues of new technology that can improve our homes, health, transportation, communication, work, lives and the planet we live on. Contextual technology is helping us explore outer space and the inner body. We have spoken to hundreds of people and looked at hundreds of technologies, and we firmly believe that adding context will make the world an easier, more efficient, cleaner and more productive place.

However, we'd be negligent if we didn't point out that the price we pay for many of these benefits is our personal privacy. Every new piece of technology we adopt requires us to consider that price and how it will be exacted. We think it is imperative to know what the companies we deal with do with the data we are required to give them.

Loss of personal privacy had been going on for a long time before Scott McNealy made his observation. In the early days of the home telephone, "party lines" enabled your neighbors to listen in to your conversations without your knowledge. Your social security number used to be a secret between you, your employer and the federal government. Now you need to share it to get a Comcast account. Your credit card numbers are stored online where they are often shared between vendors, without your knowledge. When you clicked that button to consent to a Terms of Use Agreement, you probably did not quite understand the implications hidden in the legalese.

This chipping away of personal information accelerated when we moved online, where our Facebook posts about a vacation can alert a burglar to an opportunity, and photos of a loved one may attract a stalker. In the Age of Context, mobile and wearable devices keep track of our every motion, even as we sleep, and the rate at which our privacy is eroding grows exponentially.

We did not fully understand the scope of the privacy issues people face when we started work on this book. Our goal was to tell you about incredible new technologies that can understand you well enough to predict what you will need next and to automate many mundane tasks. But with each chapter we found new privacy issues, and some are too serious to brush aside.

While we were busy searching the world for mobile, social media, sensor, data and location technologies, the issues of government surveillance became a prominent national issue in the United States. As the names Bradley (Chelsea) Manning, Dzhokhar and Tamerlan Tsarnaev,[†††] and Edward Snowden[†††] emerged from the headlines into the national consciousness, public attention came to focus on the role of the secret FISA court, the electronic surveillance of millions of Americans under a National Security Agency data-mining operation called PRISM and so much more.

We are just a couple of tech enthusiasts, and some of these national issues would normally go well beyond our purview, were it not for the fact that the same technologies we are extolling are being used to secretly watch people. Data about our searches, social media interactions and even our cell phone conversations is being collected for purposes far different than we had imagined.

Most people we talked with have strong feelings about this, as we do. But we are conflicted about a solution. We want a safer country. We want to be comfortable attending large gatherings such as the Boston Marathon. We want small cells of conspirators to be detected and deterred before they can take diabolical actions.

How much citizen privacy should be sacrificed in the name of national security? We really do not know the answer. What we have come to realize is that the conflict between security and privacy will not be easily or quickly resolved.

We do believe, however, that people would be far more comfortable if government were more transparent with the people they are supposed to serve. For example, Google wrote an open letter[†††] to Attorney General Eric Holder in June 2013, asking for permission to reveal how many of its user files had been subpoenaed under authority of the FISA court. No answer was forthcoming as of this writing. Daily revelations make us aware of more and more surveillance, resulting in less and less trust.

It leaves people wondering: Is big data watching us? The answer is a resounding "yes."

We think the benefits we gain from contextual technology are worth the cost of the loss of some of our personal information.

Not everyone will agree with us. Where there is common ground is that the public needs to be more aware of what information is being collected, and we deserve to know what will be done with that information.

Even more important, people should be allowed to opt out whenever they find that the privacy costs are just too high for their personal tastes. And it should be easy to do.

We believe that greater transparency by businesses and government will lead to higher rates of customer and citizen participation.

What bothers us is the sneaky stuff.

The Right to Go Silent

Always-on technology brings clear advantages. It is convenient to have your personal contextual assistant see that it snowed while you slept and wake you up early so you'll make it to work on time. But shouldn't there be an easy way to take a break from the relentless eyes, ears and data collectors that are part of life in the Age of Context?

Many contextual products already provide features that enable you to selectively keep some activities private. For example, NextGuide, the contextual TV program location service, lets you share what you watch and like with Facebook friends—or go private.

We have mentioned many products that offer such controls, but some of the most advanced products do not yet provide such options. We believe that both Google Glass and the Moto X phone will be flagship products in the new Age of Context, but both have features that concern us.

Glass watches what you watch. It has a sensor that records data on what you look at, how often and for how long. Moto X has a microphone that never turns off once you opt to enable it, even when the phone's power is turned off. That arrangement allows you to conveniently issue voice searches through Google Now, but it also means that the phone never stops listening. Providing the ability to selectively opt out, or go silent, is essential to earning and keeping our trust.

We call this the "Las Vegas mode." We would like to say to our Moto X, "OK Google Now, for the next three hours, do not capture anything about what we are doing."

Plain Speaking

Millions of people use Fitbit, Nike FuelBand and other devices to monitor every aspect of their bodily functions in an effort to become healthier.

The unanswered question becomes, who owns such potentially sensitive data? Who gets to share it? Some users, we are told, are so obsessed with counting every expended calorie, that they even wear the device while making love. Seems mildly amusing, until we start wondering who owns that data and who has the right to share it. Could it be used as evidence in a divorce case?

Sensors meshed together in dissolvable tattoos are used on paralyzed patients today. In the near future, those sensors are likely to monitor all sorts of bodily functions. Researchers are examining them as early detectors of cancers. Sending such data directly to our doctors makes sense. But do our insurance companies get to see it before we do? How about our employers, who often pay for most of the insurance? Who gets to decide?

From our investigation it seems the issue of personal data ownership is murky and getting murkier. Shel Israel has been a diabetic for many years, jabbing his finger a few times every day to measure his blood sugar. Every six months he brings his glucose meter to his endocrinologist, who extracts and analyzes the data.

His pharmacist recently informed him that a new California law requires him to share his data with them as well or his insurance coverage will be dropped, raising the monthly cost from about $8.25 to about $165. Who is behind this law? What is being done with medical data that is gathered at a local pharmacy and reviewed by state auditors? Israel is reasonably sure that the state's 3.7 million diabetics were not asked what they thought.

It seems self-evident that we should own our own data and that any third-party should need our permission to use it, and our refusal should not trigger financially punitive measures.

The definition of privacy as the right to be left alone should apply to more than medical records. It should apply to all data, including our photos, conversations and credit card balances. But, when we agree to those boring terms-of-use agreements, we—often unwittingly—yield to vendors the right to do with our private information whatever they wish. When you post that photo of you celebrating a bit too much on Instagram, opting to share it only with your friends, Instagram claims it has the right to reuse it—and it apparently does—but in a free society, shouldn't users be asked?

We also believe in the user's right to plain language.

If we are going to voluntarily yield personal data, then plain, straightforward language should be used in the required opt-in agreements. The repercussions should be spelled out and explained in great depth.

The loss of much of our privacy may be inevitable, but the lack of transparency is something for which we can and should hold companies accountable.

Pushing back on this point may get results faster and more easily than some people might think. But over time, we will remain the most loyal to the companies that earn our trust and do not betray it.

Human Override

EasilyDo, one of the personal contextual assistants we like, uses a "Do-It" button that gives you an opportunity to override your software assistant before it performs tasks on your behalf. Google Now, the most popular PCA, does not have the equivalent of a Do-It button. We think Google Now needs one before we can trust it with our personal information.

We told you two of the most disturbing user privacy stories we found in Chapter 9 on PCAs. First, Dave Winer talked about picking up a female friend at the airport when Google Now warned him about her delayed flight, connecting him to her flight information without any input on his part.

Then Steve Brady related a similar story where Google Now presumed he was in a more advanced stage of a relationship with a woman he knew than was actually the case and the mobile app started sharing her private data as if they were committed partners.

For users to trust Google Now in the long run, the danger of personal contextual assistants giving out privileged information must be far less than the threat of a human assistant doing so.

All personal contextual assistants should be designed to ask for permission and not make assumptions, until a user pattern is well established and the owner specifically grants certain permissions that would remain in effect until cancelled. Further, they should provide a means for correcting inaccurate assumptions or information.

No one wants a PCA that rats you out. You cannot fire them the way you would an indiscreet employee, but you can stop using them and stop trusting their manufacturer.

Privacy Is Subjective

Privacy is complex, fluid and granular. How much of it we want depends on many variables. Facebook used to let people respond to their relationship status as "It's complicated." We think the same option can be used for privacy.

As parents, we would be willing to yield a lot of our children's location and personal data if it would ease their suffering from diabetes or asthma as we talked about in our chapter on Contextual Health.

However, we may not want a security sensor that can record data or movement in our bedrooms. We may not mind Facebook electing to share a cute picture of our kid at a school concert, but most people would not want photos of their children in front of their houses where addresses are visible posted in public spaces.

Such user-empowering controls are not technically hard to accomplish. As contextual technology pushes forward with relentless speed of development, certain safeguards seem to be getting overlooked or bypassed.

For example, if a college student posts a photo showing how he over-celebrated at a graduation party, technology exists for an online service to display a pop-up dialogue box to ask: "Are you sure you want to post this? This photo may be harmful to you in a job interview, or when you ask your parents to subsidize your summer vacation..."

Warnings about risks seem to have been brushed aside in recent times, even though we are entering increasingly risky times. In the Age of Context we seem to be unnecessarily performing risky tasks without a safety net.

Trust Is the New Currency

We believe the most trustworthy companies will thrive in the Age of Context, and those found to be short on candor will end up short on customers. Transparency and trustworthiness will be the differentiating factors by which customers will make an increasing number of choices.

Most of the products we have examined in this book have one or more competitors already; the remainder soon will. Competitors will leapfrog each other's capabilities—whenever one product offers a desirable new feature, the others will soon offer a similar or slightly better one.

In mobile phones, iPhone had a clear functionality edge for a long time, but as we write this, Android has equaled or surpassed iPhone's features. Now Moto X has come along, which may set a whole new standard because it has incorporated contextual functionality into its operating system.

The key point is that despite the volatile nature of the market, many products will become commodities earlier in their development cycles than was the case with previous technologies. For example, we looked at about ten PCAs. Each of those we highlighted had at least one unique feature, but it seemed likely that competitors would be able to match them pretty easily. People will probably choose just one PCA and stick with it, even if one feature lags for a few months. The same tendency for people to commit to one product and stick with it affects wearable devices and home management systems.

If features aren't the deciding factor, how will we choose? We think that most people will select the products made by the companies they trust the most. The most transparent companies—the ones that give the user privacy options they can understand and the option to turn apps and devices off and on as they see fit—will be deemed the most trustworthy. Similarly, companies whose products warn users before they do something that might embarrass them will be valued and trusted, gaining the customers' loyalty along the way.

Today, Google seems to have taken a leadership position in this area. They have posted a single page[†††] where you can see the company's privacy policy as well as all the types of data it collects on users. If you visit that page, you may be surprised at how much Google knows about you. Makes you wonder what data all the companies not posting similar pages have on you, doesn't it?

Although Google may lead in this area today, the previously mentioned serious and unresolved Glass and Moto X privacy issues are evidence that every company has at least one Achilles' heel in the area of privacy.

If we were developing a long-term company strategy for the Contextual Age, we would start by matching everything Google has done in transparency, and then try to surpass it. Users would certainly embrace such a competition.

We think business leadership, in the short term, will require understanding that more is gained than lost by shining some sunlight on a few shady areas. Some organizational decision makers have grown comfortable and have prospered in the shadows. Some may opt to lurk there. But that's not where their customers are comfortable. And ultimately, profitability lies in the customers' comfort zone.

In our view, the shadow-lurkers may grab some sweet, low-hanging fruit, but in the long run they will lose to companies like Google and other transparent entities. Openness and transparency create a significant opportunity for every startup that has giant-killing already etched into its organizational DNA. If we are right, then the Age of Context will give us an open new world

Reunion: 2038

I never think of the future—it comes soon enough.

Albert Einstein

I t's 7:30 AM, September 16, 2038, when a little voice goes off inside Robert Scoble's head. He is sleeping blissfully in his Napa County home near his vineyards. The comfortable two-story home was the only significant change he made in his lifestyle 25 years ago after Age of Context became a runaway best seller, topping all charts and being read by over 2 million people in more than 50 countries.

Sales had resulted in prosperity for Scoble and Shel Israel that neither had anticipated. It didn't much change either of them. Scoble kept traveling the world to interview technologists who pushed the envelope, and Israel continued to write a lot and consult a little.

Both of them now own clean-energy, high-performance cars that they could not previously afford. Israel and his wife of 41 years, Paula, travel a bit more and Scoble uses some of his surprise wealth to acquire every new tech gadget that catches his fancy. Both give regularly to worthy causes, their favorite being charity:water.[†††]

Scoble's eponymous Scobleizer Winery produces only a few hundred bottles each year; enough for holiday gifts and many dinners with friends. Inexpensive sensors and robots make tending the grapes easy and every October the Scobles throw a big "harvest & stomp" party. Most of the attendees are young entrepreneurs intent on changing the world.

On this morning, Scoble is dreaming about 2013, when the book first appeared, how it got people and businesses to understand the promise of the new Age of Context, even as it ignited a 25-year debate over privacy and data ownership. It is a fitting dream for the day—the 25ᵗʰ anniversary of *Age of Context's* publication.

"Good morning, Robert," says the voice in his head. "Today is September 16. It is 71 degrees Fahrenheit in your backyard and it is expected to rise to 83 at 3:00 PM. You have only two appointments: a call with Shel Israel at noon and an afternoon and dinner with Marc Benioff at the Ritz-Carlton in Half Moon Bay. Traffic to the Ritz is clear all the way, except for the usual tie-ups on the Golden Gate Bridge and Doyle Drive."

The voice was literally emanating from inside Scoble's head. A few weeks earlier he had become one of the first to beta test the new Google Everywhere visual computer. The nearly microscopic device had been connected directly to his optic nerve, enabling him to communicate not by old-fashioned gestures or voice commands, but by brainwaves.

Back in 2013, Salesforce.com founder and CEO Marc Benioff had mentioned brainwaves in his foreword to the book. In 2013, using brainwaves to give machines commands was still in the experimental stage. At MIT, they got a robot to fetch a cup of coffee. Brain-interactive prosthetic limbs were just starting to operate effectively on a few pioneering volunteers. A few years later, technologists realized that brainwaves were the fastest way to interact with machines. The greatest issue was getting people to focus when they send a mental command. Machine learning still has trouble following humans whose minds tend to drift from the subject at hand.

Google Everywhere is the culmination of a 25-year evolution from Google Glass, now a museum artifact that kids laugh at because the device seems clumsy in design and severely limited in functionality.

Over the years, digital eyewear became integrated into regular glasses, with sensors embedded into the lenses. A few years later, the device became a set of contact lenses. Many who needed no visual corrections adopted lenses just to be able to use the device. Now, digital eyewear is more popular than the old smartphones had ever been, and far less expensive. Most people on Earth had some form of digital eyewear, with older models being sold for just a few dollars through Amazon.com or eBay.

Even in 2038, most people remain queasy about having microscopic devices installed inside their bodies. Israel had already declared that the embedded opticals were several steps over his personal freaky line. Some people are still a little retro. Israel, now on his 11th book, still uses an old-fashioned keypad that attaches to his external eyewear through Wifi.

Several very large companies offer many digital eyewear choices in a wide range styles and prices, and they evolved to become the central personal contextual assistants in most people's lives. They connect with other wearable devices and are powered by batteries that are often contained in clothing and charged automatically by Wifi. They also connect with wristbands that monitor every possible bodily function.

The PCAs also are in constant contact with household sensors that monitor every imaginable environmental factor, from pesky insects on the patio to excessive ozone radiation. Because Scoble's PCA is directly connected to his brain, he can monitor every possible data bit whenever he wishes—and filter them out when he does not.

But there is a tradeoff: In the old days, a privacy issue flashpoint had been that the old Google Glass monitored what people watched; now Google Everywhere monitors what they think. Although Glass came to know Scoble better than even his spouse, Everywhere knows him better than he knows himself.

Even before Scoble rises on this fine September morning, his optical PCA starts executing a series of commands in and around his home. Outdoor windows reduce tint to let in warm sunshine while filtering out damaging rays. Shower water starts heating precisely four minutes before the system expects him to step in. His coffee maker begins brewing extra-strong precisely to his tastes.

As Scoble steps in, the shower water automatically comes down at precisely the temperature and pressure he usually enjoys. If it had been Maryam, the water would be three degrees warmer. If Scoble just thinks the water is too warm, Everywhere reads the thought and signals the contextual shower to cool it just a bit.

As Scoble brushes his teeth, Everywhere gets a message from his toothbrush that it is time for a cleaning. After getting Scoble's permission, his optical device contacts his dentist's office and compares schedules; without any human involvement, a good time slot is reserved.

His optical PCA has already shared his calendar and the weather with his smart closet mirror, which offers Scoble a few good choices to wear to his reunion. He picks a solid blue shirt, as he so very often does.

Clothing looks similar to the styles of 25 years ago, but these new garments are quite different. For one thing, they use nanotechnology to self-clean. The fabric's weave opens and closes depending on weather and Scoble's body temperature.

Scoble is now 74, and Israel has recently observed his 94th birthday. Both are still going strong, as are a great many people their age. Doctors predict that most people living today will reach their 120th birthday, although few have yet reached that age. Lots of people plan to work at least until their 100th birthday, including Scoble and Israel. Contextual medicine, which has evolved from a grassroots movement to be embraced by a majority of mainstream scientists, technologists, patients and doctors, has managed to eliminate many of the diseases and environmental hazards that were prevalent back in 2013.

Thanks to contextual technology more people keep fitter than ever before. Artificial limbs are almost impossible to distinguish from the body parts they replaced. The once-cumbersome exoskeletons used by paraplegics in the old days have been refined so that they are now integrated into specialized apparel.

Taking It to the Ritz

In his foreword, Benioff, who remains chairman of Salesforce.com, had lamented how much better hotels could serve guest needs if they would just adopt contextual technology. By odd coincidence, he used almost the same words Scoble used a few chapters later when he pointed to the Ritz-Carlton near his old home in Half Moon Bay as an example of a business's missed opportunity for upselling.

After the book came out, the three became friends. When Israel and Scoble decided in 2014 to meet for a first anniversary dinner, the authors invited Benioff. Scoble immediately suggested the Ritz in Half Moon Bay as the venue. They've been returning there on the anniversary date ever since.

This 2038 reunion is the first time that one of them would be absent. Israel was visiting Armstrongville, the first Mars settlement—named for the first Earthling to walk on the moon. Settling Mars was made possible when sensors on NASA's rover *Curiosity II* discovered steam vents on the red planet that led to an enormous underground fresh water ocean—enough to sustain life and people. When the smart-domed city was completed and populated by scientists and engineers in 2025, NASA called for 3000 civilian volunteers to settle the red planet. More than 100,000 signed up. Monthly commercial flights had started just six months before Israel took off. It was a grueling and expensive five-day flight.

Adventurous travelers had to sign up over a year in advance, and then take the time slot they were assigned. Israel was forced to skip the reunion— he was flying on a press pass and had to take the flight he was assigned to or wait a long time for another opportunity. The trip fulfilled a lifetime dream. His love for science and technology began when he read *The Martian Chronicles* as a schoolboy.

Scoble took one last sip of coffee and sent a thought signal to have his robotic maid clear the dishes. He took a last contented look at his ripening grapes and thought, "Okay, Tesla. Pick me up."

Seventy-five feet away, a garage door rolled open and his silver Tesla Model X Gen 17 rolled up to his front door. The car, recognizing its owner, unlocked the door and adjusted the seat.

He slid onto the seat. "Okay Tesla. Take me to the Ritz," he thought. The engine hummed to life and the car rolled easily along back roads for a couple of miles and then south onto Highway 29. When it reached Highway 37, the Tesla turned west.

As the car was keeping itself at precisely the speed limit, Scoble had time to reflect. Lately, he was not turning on his social networks as frequently as he had when he was younger, and the way billions of younger people constantly did. He told Everywhere he wanted some soft jazz, which poured out of the Tesla's 16 surround sound speakers. Over the years, Scoble had come to agree with Israel's often-repeated comment: "Sometimes, always on is too much."

A few miles away, Benioff had enjoyed a similar morning. He, too, was enjoying an automatic ride to Half Moon Bay.

As scheduled, Benioff, Scoble and Israel joined in a holographic conference call. Each saw images of the other two standing in front of them. They talked about old times and outer space. They talked about grandchildren and pets. Reception wasn't bad considering that 35 million miles of outer space separated Israel from his old friends.

A short while later, the two cars arrive almost simultaneously at the Ritz, delivering their passengers to the main entrance and then parking themselves in the guest lot. As the two friends enter the lobby, they are welcomed by name and wished a hearty congratulations on the anniversary of the book's publication.

Scoble and Benioff enter the Navio Restaurant and are seated at their usual table where two glasses of 25-year-old Oban Whiskey are waiting for them.

They toast the book. They toast each other. They toast Israel and they toast the Ritz for finally getting context right.

Parting Thought

This chapter is, of course, a little flight of fantasy. Many of our predictions here probably will not happen. But many will. We just don't know which will be which.

We have written *Age of Context* with excitement and with pain. We are excited because contextual technology can solve so many of the world's problems. We are pained by the damage that abuse could cause.

At the end of the day, the technology has always been and always will be just a set of tools for people to use or abuse as they see fit. We can gush about the virtues or agonize about the dangers until we turn purple.

What the Age of Context will look like 25 years from now is really up to us.

Links In This Book

Introduction

Forbes	http://www.forbes.com/sites/shelisrael/
Naked Conversations: How Blogs are Changing the Way Businesses Talk with Customers	http://www.amazon.com/ Naked-Conversations-Changing- Businesses-Customers/ dp/047174719X
Cray-1 supercomputer that cost $8.8 million	https://www.google.com/#bav=on.2,or.r_ cp.r_qf.&fp=8d6fb6129acf7a
Starner's Google+ page	https://plus.google. com/105804767481830727070/about
Starner's doctoral thesis	http://citeseerx.ist.psu.edu/viewdoc/ download?doi=10.1.1.35.8499& rep=rep1&type=pdf
The Perfect Storm	http://en.wikipedia.org/wiki/ The_Perfect_Storm_(book)
Jim Gray	http://research.microsoft.com/en-us/um/ people/gray/

Chapter 1

Number of cellphones surpassed the number of people	http://techcrunch.com/2012/02/14/the-number-of-mobile-devices-will-exceed-worlds-population-by-2012-other-shocking-figures/
Cellphones to grow to 665 million by 2016	http://techcrunch.com/2012/04/10/gartner-tablets-apple-ipad-dominate/
Google Glass	http://www.google.com/glass/start/
Juniper Research estimate of wearable computing revenue	http://www.businessinsider.com/this-is-what-apples-curved-glass-iwatch-might-look-like-2013-2#ixzz2LC54uFDt
Macheen	http://www.macheen.com/
ItsOn	http://www.itsoninc.com/
T-Mobile	http://www.t-mobile.com/
Sprint	http://sprint.com/
Gartner on number of apps downloaded	http://www.gartner.com/newsroom/id/2153215
Naked Conversations	http://amzn.to/Naked-Conversations
A billion tweets per day	http://www.mediabistro.com/alltwitter/tag/tweets-per-day
Nearly 1.5 billion people on social networks	http://searchenginewatch.com/article/2167518/Worldwide-Social-Media-Usage-Trends-in-2012
Eric Schmidt	http://www.forbes.com/profile/eric-schmidt/
Size of the internet	http://news.softpedia.com/news/How-Big-Is-the-Internet-10177.shtml
Expand by half the size it was in 2005	http://www.internetworldstats.com/emarketing.htm

90% of world's data created in last two years	http://www-01.ibm.com/software/data/bigdata/
Rick Smolan	http://en.wikipedia.org/wiki/Rick_Smolan
The Human Face of Big Data	http://humanfaceofbigdata.com/
Page Rank	http://en.wikipedia.org/wiki/PageRank
Social Graph	http://en.wikipedia.org/wiki/Social_graph
Graph Search	https://www.facebook.com/about/graphsearch
Neo Technology	http://www.neotechnology.com/
Picture is worth a thousand words	http://en.wikipedia.org/wiki/A_picture_is_worth_a_thousand_words
ai-one, inc.	http://www.ai-one.com/about-ai-one/
Searching for ideas	http://www.ai-one.com/2013/01/18/big-data-solutions-intelligent-agents-find-meaning-of-text/
The Filter Bubble	http://www.thefilterbubble.com/
Rackspace video work	http://scobleizer.com/
Kevin Ashton	http://en.wikipedia.org/wiki/Kevin_Ashton
Internet of Things	http://en.wikipedia.org/wiki/Internet_of_Things
Highlight	https://plus.google.com/+Scobleizer/posts/DwiEbMwAxGj
Where your keys are	http://www.amazon.com/s/?ie=UTF8&keywords=find+your+keys
Who your dog likes	http://www.oes.org/page2/3187~Cool_invention_for_Dogs_from_MIT.html

Sensors in prosthetic hands	http://www.independent.co.uk/life-style/ gadgets-and-tech/news/a-sensational- breakthrough-the-first-bionic-hand-that-can- feel-8498622.html
Tohoku earthquake and tsunami	http://en.wikipedia.org/ wiki/2011_T%C5%8Dhoku_earthquake_and_ tsunami
Shark Net	http://www.wired.co.uk/news/ archive/2012-08/21/shark-location-app
Sensors in body armor	http://www.homelandsecuritynewswire. com/us-army-emphasizes-new-body- armor?page=0,2
Sensors to detect lameness in racehorses	http://research.missouri.edu/news/2012/ horse_sensor.php
GreenGoose	http://www.crunchbase.com/company/ greengoose
Sensors magazine	http://www.sensorsmag.com/ melanie-martella
Sensor fusion	http://en.wikipedia.org/wiki/Sensor_fusion
Caterina Fake	http://en.wikipedia.org/wiki/Caterina_Fake
Findery	https://findery.com/
Daniel Graf	https://plus.google. com/102081466907669508480/posts
Kyte	http://www.crunchbase.com/company/kyte
Galapagos Islands	https://www.google.com/search?q=Google+ Maps+galapagos&oq=Google+Maps+galapag os&aqs=chrome.0.57j0l3j64.6818j0&sourceid =chrome&ie=UTF-8#q=Google+Maps+galap agos&source=univ&tbm=

Foursquare	https://foursquare.com/
Over 20 million registered Foursquare users	http://en.wikipedia.org/wiki/Foursquare
Massachusetts Home Show	http://www.jenksproductions.com/masshomeshow.html

Chapter 2

Amber Naslund	http://www.brasstackthinking.com/about/
Sidera Works	http://SideraWorks.com
Skydivers leapt from a blimp	http://www.youtube.com/watch?v=uh-liQDE3cM
If I had Glass	http://www.google.com/glass/start/how-to-get-one/
Jolie O'Dell declared	http://venturebeat.com/2013/05/09/google-glass-hands-on-review/
Five Point Cafe	http://ivn.us/2013/05/06/as-google-glass-nears-release-legal-problems-arise/
Gary Howell	http://en.wikipedia.org/wiki/Gary_Howell
Illegal surveillance device	http://ivn.us/2013/05/06/as-google-glass-nears-release-legal-problems-arise/
Jeff Bercovici	http://www.forbes.com/sites/jeffbercovici/
Glass would make classroom cheating rampant	http://www.forbes.com/sites/jeffbercovici/2012/09/26/if-you-think-cheating-is-rampant-now-just-wait-till-google-glasses-are-here/
Glass banned in theaters	http://variety.com/2013/digital/news/google-glass-nato-theater-ban-1200479394/

The Urban Dictionary	http://www.urbandictionary.com/
Glasshole	http://www.urbandictionary.com/define. php?term=Glasshole
Steve Mann	http://en.wikipedia.org/wiki/Steve_Mann
He was enjoying lunch at a McDonald's	http://www.huffingtonpost.com/2012/07/17/ steve-mann-attacked-paris-mcdonalds-digital-eye-glass-photos_n_1680263.html
Oakley	http://www.oakley.com/
Airwave	http://www.oakley.com/airwave
Scoble making presentations at tech conferences	https://plus.google.com/+Scobleizer/posts/ bwigmL7TWqv
First review to Google+	https://plus.google.com/+Scobleizer/posts/ ZLV9GdmkRzS
Maryam	https://www.facebook.com/maryamie
Photographed him in the shower	http://venturebeat.com/2013/04/28/heres-robert-scoble-showering-with-google-glass/
Peter Shankman	http://shankman.com/ if-google-glass-fails-its-robert-scobles-fault/
Larry Page	https://plus.google.com/+LarryPage/posts
SRI International	http://www.sri.com/
Tamarine	http://www.tamarinerestaurant.com/
Supun Samarasekera	http://www.sri.com/about/people/ supun-samarasekera
Showed us a pair of augmented reality binoculars	http://youtu.be/AY2H3EBglDo

Terracotta Army	http://en.wikipedia.org/wiki/Terracotta_Army
Brainwaves controlling robot demonstrated	http://news.discovery.com/tech/videos/tech-mind-controlled-robot-uses-human-brainwaves.htm
3D holograms hover in the air	http://en.wikipedia.org/wiki/Computer-generated_holography
Arthur C. Clarke wrote	http://www.famousquotes.com/author/arthur-c-clarke/
Saturday Night Live skit	http://www.youtube.com/watch?v=PyI8rP6XtX8
Rosa Golijan	https://plus.google.com/+RosaGolijan/posts
Stefan Weitz	http://www.crunchbase.com/person/stefan-weitz
HIS, Inc.	http://www.ihs.com/products/global-insight/index.aspx
Glass will retail for about $400	http://www.technologyreview.com/news/511776/google-wants-to-install-a-computer-on-your-face/
Frogger	http://www.happyhopper.org/
Archeologists controlling a drone	http://www.theguardian.com/world/2013/aug/25/peru-archaeologists-drones-ancient-ruins
Pairasight, Inc.	http://www.pairasight.com
Christopher Salow	http://www.linkedin.com/pub/chris-salow/8/25b/716
Aaron Salow	http://www.linkedin.com/pub/c-aaron-salow/8/20a/584

Epiphany Eyewear	http://www.epiphanyeyewear.com/
Recon Instruments	http://www.reconinstruments.com
Recon Jet	http://www.engadget.com/2013/05/15/ recon-instruments-reveals-recon-jet/
Bill Geiser	http://www.linkedin.com/in/billgeiser
MetaWatch	http://www.metawatch.org/
"look like the Borg"	http://en.wikipedia.org/wiki/ Borg_(Star_Trek)
Basketball players wearing eyeglass frames without lenses	http://www.businessinsider.com/ russell-westbrook-red-glasses-2012-5
Warby Parker	http://www.warbyparker.com
LensCrafters	http://www.lenscrafters.com/
Memoto	http://memoto.com/
acquired a facial recognition company in 2010	http://techcrunch.com/2010/08/20/ its-official-google-acquires-like-com/
Steve Lee	http://techcrunch.com/2010/08/20/ its-official-google-acquires-like-com/
Glass was hacked twice	http://www.npr.org/blogs/ alltechconsidered/2013/07/17/202725167/ clever-hacks-give-google-glass-many- unintended-powers

Chapter 3

Cheers Theme Song	http://en.wikipedia.org/wiki/Cheers
Sam Lessin	http://www.crunchbase.com/person/ sam-lessin

Lessin was born in 1914

https://www.facebook.com/pages/
Sam-Lessin/157309034334272

Facebook Timeline

http://mashable.com/category/
facebook-timeline/

Vidya Narayanan

www.linkedin.com/in/hellovidya

Qualcomm

http://www.qualcomm.com

Gimbal

https://www.gimbal.com

Person of Interest

http://www.imdb.com/title/tt1839578/

NFL took in $9.5 billion in revenue

http://www.plunkettresearch.com/
sports-recreation-leisure-market-research/
industry-statistics

Jonathan Kraft

http://en.wikipedia.org/wiki/Jonathan_Kraft

KirschWords blog

http://blog.patriots.com/category/
kirsch-words/

Patriots team website

http://patriots.com/

Enterasys Secure Networks

http://www.enterasys.com/

Vala Afshar

https://twitter.com/ValaAfshar

Highlight

http://highlig.ht/

Maribel Lopez

http://www.forbes.com/sites/maribellopez/

Lopez Research

http://www.lopezresearch.com/

MagicBand

http://www.nbcnews.com/technology/
disneylands-wireless-wristband-could-
replace-tickets-1C6309090

VinTank

http://www.vintank.com/

Paul Mabray	http://www.vintank.com/about-vintank/the-team/paul-mabray/
James Jory	http://www.vintank.com/about-vintank/the-team/james-jory/
Craig Camp	http://winecampblog.com/
Cornerstone Cellars	http://www.cornerstonecellars.com/
Opus One	http://www.opusonewinery.com/
Marc Andreessen	http://www.crunchbase.com/person/marc-andreessen
EasyPay	http://www.wired.com/gadgetlab/2011/11/apple-store-app-updated-to-allow-self-checkout-personal-pickup/
PrimeSense	http://www.primesense.com/about/contact/
Microsoft Kinect	http://www.xbox.com/en-US/KINECT
Aviad Maizels	http://www.youtube.com/watch?v=OAPBVyB0Cpw
Shopperception	http://www.shopperception.com/
Wal-Mart	http://www.stores.org/2012/Top-100-Retailers#.UTI9W-vEakI
Heineken the world's sixth most popular beer	http://www.huffingtonpost.com/2012/09/26/worlds-most-popular-beer_n_1914327.html
Ariel Di Stefano	https://twitter.com/arieldistefano
Verge reported on Cara camera	http://www.theverge.com/2013/5/20/4341388/imrsv-rolls-out-cheap-face-detection-software-cara
IMRSV	https://imrsv.com/

Andreessen Horowitz   http://a16z.com/

Chapter 4

Bob Lutz   http://en.wikipedia.org/wiki/
Bob_Lutz_(businessman)

FastCompany Interview   http://www.fastcompany.com/1569709/
gms-bob-lutz-talks-social-media-and-global-
warming

Fastlane   http://fastlane.gmblogs.com/

John M. Broder   http://topics.nytimes.com/topics/reference/
timestopics/people/b/john_m_broder/index.
html

Tesla Model S   http://www.teslamotors.com/models

Tesla carried away on the back of a
tow truck   http://graphics8.nytimes.
com/images/2013/02/10/
automobiles/10JPTESL1/10JPTESL1-
articleLarge-v2.jpg

Broder reported having had a very
bad experience   http://www.nytimes.com/2013/02/10/
automobiles/stalled-on-the-ev-highway.
html?ref=automobiles&_r=0

Elon Musk   http://www.forbes.com/profile/elon-musk

Event Data Recorder (EDR)   http://en.wikipedia.org/wiki/
Event_data_recorder

The National Highway Safety Council
is lobbying   http://www.mydaytondailynews.
com/news/business/car-black-
boxes-could-become-mandatory/
nXsGS/

Musk posted graphs   http://www.teslamotors.com/blog/
most-peculiar-test-drive

Margaret Sullivan

http://publiceditor.blogs.nytimes.com/
author/margaret-sullivan/

K. Venkatesh Prasad

http://media.ford.com/article_display.
cfm?article_id=31396

eToyota Division of North America

http://www.toyota-global.com/company/
history_of_toyota/75years/data/business/
it-its_e-toyota-gazoo/e-toyota-gazoo.html

Vic Gundotra

http://www.crunchbase.com/person/
vic-gundotra

Gundotra in a Mercedes video ad

http://www.youtube.com/
watch?v=5XXypu3dVPM

A man with a sawed-off shotgun
approached

http://latimesblogs.latimes.com/
technology/2009/10/onstar-gps-carjacking.
html

GM OnStar system

http://en.wikipedia.org/wiki/OnStar

Stolen Vehicle Slowdown feature

https://www.onstar.com/web/portal/
securityexplore?tab=1&seo=goo_|_
GM+OnStar_|_RTN-OnStar+Security-
Broad_|_Stolen+Vehicle+Slowdown_|_onstar
stolen vehicle slowdown

Basis wristband

http://www.mybasis.com/

MyKey encourages safety

http://media.ford.com/article_display.
cfm?article_id=29172

Glympse

http://www.glympse.com/

Install EDR black boxes

http://autos.yahoo.com/blogs/motoramic/
car-black-boxes-becoming-standard-raising-
privacy-hackles-175356232.html

Wisconsin passed the first seat belt
requirement

http://en.wikipedia.org/wiki/
Seat_belt_legislation

Spotify.com

https://www.spotify.com/us/

Google Calendar

https://www.google.com/calendar/render

Test-driving a 2011 Ford Escape
Hybrid

http://globalneighbourhoods.net/2010/08/
ford-escape-hybrid-a-review.html

Loaner featured a SYNC automated
system

http://www.ford.com/technology/sync/

Ford's Prasad champions this concept

http://media.ford.com/article_display.
cfm?article_id=31396

Twist is "call-ahead" software

http://itunes.apple.com/us/app/twist/
id449988837?mt=8

Gasbuddy.com

http://gasbuddy.com

Nooly Micro Weather

https://itunes.apple.com/us/app/
nooly-micro-weather/id495150606?mt=8

Waze

http://www.waze.com

American teens prefer owning a
smartphone to a car

http://www.intomobile.com/2011/11/22/
todays-teenagers-prefer-owning-iphone-
owning-car-proof-theyre-worst-generation-
ever/

The U.S. Department of
Transportation reports

http://www.pothole.info/2010/06/young-
people-driving-less-now-%E2%80%93-but-
what-about-in-5-to-10-years/

Zipcar

http://www.zipcar.com/sf/
campaign?gclid=CMS27pHohrYCFcZ_
Qgod8T0A9g

TechShop

http://www.techshop.ws/

Chapter 5

Vehicles with odd spinning devices	http://www.youtube.com/watch?v=VAiH1LX8guk
Aerometric	http://www.aerometric.com/services/lidar/
Velodyne	http://velodynelidar.com/lidar/lidar.aspx
Self-driving car chugged along	http://www.youtube.com/watch?v=cdgQpa1pUUE
Mahan told a news reporter	http://idealab.talkingpointsmemo.com/2012/03/google-video-demonstrates-self-driving-car-with-legally-blind-driver.php
Lidar unit cost $70,000	http://en.wikipedia.org/wiki/Google_driverles_car
An Audi YouTube clip	http://www.youtube.com/watch?v=sjcvai2xcaQ
Annie Lien	http://www.linkedin.com/in/annielien/
Volkswagen Group Electronics Research Lab	http://www.vwerl.com/
Scott Monty	http://www.linkedin.com/in/scottmonty
a driverless, lidar-less Audi A7	http://www.nytimes.com/2013/05/28/science/on-the-road-in-mobileyes-self-driving-car.html?_r=0
Mobileye Vision Technologies	http://www.mobileye.com/

Chapter 6

Greg Lindsay	http://www.greglindsay.org/about/

University of Illinois at Urbana-Champaign	http://illinois.edu/
Multiple reports show cities population surging	http://usnews.nbcnews.com/_news/2013/05/23/18441345-urban-renewal-census-figures-show-cities-surging?lite
U.S. Census Bureau	http://usnews.nbcnews.com/_news/2013/05/23/18441345-urban-renewal-census-figures-show-cities-surging?lite
Brookings Institution	http://www.brookings.edu/research/opinions/2012/06/29-cities-suburbs-frey
Youngstown, Ohio	http://www.cleveland.com/business/index.ssf/2010/01/youngstown_makes_strides_towar.html
America's most miserable city	http://reason.com/blog/2010/03/04/cleveland-is-officially-the-mo
Allison Peltz	http://www.linkedin.com/in/allisonpeltz
$3.6 trillion for infrastructure repair	http://www.popularmechanics.com/technology/engineering/infrastructure/4301580
Jonathan Mark	http://www.linkedin.com/pub/jonathan-mark/48/241/722
Big Dig	http://en.wikipedia.org/wiki/Big_Dig
Autodesk	http://www.autodesk.com/
Doug Eberhard	http://www.linkedin.com/pub/doug-eberhard/5/152/a76
Parsons Brinckerhoff	http://www.pbworld.com/
Herman Hollerith	http://en.wikipedia.org/wiki/Herman_Hollerith

Thomas J. Watson

http://en.wikipedia.org/wiki/
Thomas_J_Watson

Smarter Planet

http://www.ibm.com/smarterplanet/us/
en/?ca=v_smarterplanet

Identify criminal hot spots

http://www-03.ibm.com/press/us/en/
pressrelease/32169.wss

Reduced pollution

http://www-03.ibm.com/press/us/en/
pressrelease/27813.wss

Understand how adverse patterns
develop

http://www.ibm.com/smarterplanet/us/en/
leadership/hamiltoncounty/

Howard School of Academics and
Technology

http://www.hcde.org/hamilton-
county-schools/high-schools/
howard-school-of-academics-and-technology

Bitcarrier

http://www.bitcarrier.com/aboutus

Ricardo Fernandez

http://www.linkedin.com/in/
ricardofernandez

Libelium

http://www.libelium.com

IBM SmartCamp

http://ibmsmartcamp.com/

Alicia Asin

http://www.linkedin.com/in/aliciaasin

Following the 2011 nuclear disaster

http://www.world-nuclear.org/info/
Safety-and-Security/Safety-of-Plants/
Fukushima-Accident-2011/

Nooly

http://www.nooly.com/

Yaron Reich

http://www.nooly.com/about-us/
management-2/

Waze

http://www.waze.com/

Model planes	http://www.wired.com/dangerroom/2012/06/ff_drones/all/
Maker movement online magazine	http://makezine.com/
Maker Faires	http://makerfaire.com/
TechShop	http://www.techshop.ws/
Mark Hatch	http://www.techshop.ws/founders.html
Guided us through the 17,000-square-foot San Francisco facility	http://www.youtube.com/watch?v=88vTsKdysoo
Identical to the other five	http://www.techshop.ws/locations.html
Square, Inc.	https://squareup.com/
DODOcase	http://www.dodocase.com/
Clustered Systems	http://www.clusteredsystems.com/
Driptech	http://www.driptech.com/
Brian Burling	https://plus.google.com/110719587488168536383/posts
eMotimo	http://www.emotimo.com/
As Scoble wrote in a blog post	http://www.youtube.com/watch?v=88vTsKdysoo

Chapter 7

Robert Orben	http://www.coolnsmart.com/author/robert_orben/
Health sensors will be a $5.6 billion market	http://mobihealthnews.com/21878/mobile-health-sensor-market-to-hit-5-6b-by-2017/

Proteus Digital Health	http://proteusdigitalhealth.com
An average of 130,000 Americans die each year	http://www.reuters.com/ article/2012/07/25/us-heart-patients-meds-idUSBRE86O16M20120725
Proteus being tested	http://blogs.nature.com/news/2012/07/ digital-pills-make-their-way-to-market.html
Luddite	http://en.wikipedia.org/wiki/Luddite
Fitbit	http://www.fitbit.com/one
Nike+ Fuelband	http://store.nike.com/us/en_us/pd/fuelband/ pid-691776/pgid-670534
Six million users in May 2013	http://nikeinc.com/news/nike-unveils-revolutionary-nike-experience-for-basketball-and-training-athletes
Basis	http://www.mybasis.com/
Quantified Self	http://quantifiedself.com/
Won't need a doctor	http://www.youtube.com/ watch?v=yTtL-iAXJxo
Loic Le Meur	http://www.crunchbase.com/person/ loic-le-meur
LeWeb	http://www.leweb.co/
Application Programming Interface (API)	http://loiclemeur.com/english/2010/08/ writing-apps-for-your-tv-is-cool-but-nothing-compared-to-your-body-api-where-is-the-ibody-appstore.html
Endomondo Sports Tracker	https://play.google.com/store/apps/ details?id=com.endomondo.android&hl=en
Keas	http://keas.com/

Adam Bosworth	http://www.crunchbase.com/person/adam-bosworth
Dr. Jennifer Dyer	http://twitter.com/EndoGoddess
EndoGoal	http://www.endogoal.com/
Vivienne Ming	http://www.vivienneming.com/
Gild	http://www.gild.com/company/
Omnipod Insulin Pump	https://www.myomnipod.com/PPCDemoPodConditionsAgreement/?gclid=CKPPqLLB-LYCFYN7QgodbQ8A1w
Dexcom 4	http://www.dexcom.com/dexcom-g4-platinum
Woman 2.0 conference	http://www.women2.com/pitch-sf-conference-2013/
More than 9% of children in the U.S. have asthma	http://www.aafa.org/display.cfm?id=8&sub=42
About nine people die from asthma daily	www.cdc.gov/vitalsigns/asthma/
Annual cost of asthma is $50 billion	http://www.upi.com/Health_News/2012/05/01/Medical-costs-of-asthma-about-50-billion/UPI-57541335927000/
Asthmapolis	http://asthmapolis.com/
Whitney Zatzkin	http://twitter.com/MsWZ
TedMed Conference	http://www.tedmed.com/
Geomedicine	http://www.informationweek.com/healthcare/mobile-wireless/geo-medicine-new-frontier-in-medical-inf/240001727

Bill Davenhall   http://www.ted.com/speakers/bill_davenhall.
                                    html

Esri   http://www.esri.com

Wearable Technologies   http://www.wearable-technologies.
                                    com/2011/06/wt-for-an-aging-population/

Vega Everon   http://www.everon.fi/en/products/
                                    hardwares/vega/

Tunstall Vi   http://americas.tunstall.com/

BodyTel   http://is.jrc.ec.europa.eu/pages/TFS/
                                    documents/BodyTel.pdf

uChek   https://itunes.apple.com/us/app/uchek/
                                    id638063128?mt=8

Tattoo-like electronic mesh   http://www.technologyreview.com/
                                    news/512061/electronic-sensors-printed-
                                    directly-on-the-skin/

Feed herself chocolates   http://medcitynews.com/2012/12/prosthetic-
                                    arm-controlled-by-brainwaves-allows-
                                    quadraplegic-woman-to-feed-herself/

Beam   http://www.gizmag.com/
                                    beam-toothbrush-bluetooth/21489/

Phillips   http://www.usa.philips.com/c/
                                    Electric-Toothbrushes/139863/cat/

IntelligentM   http://www.intelligentm.com/

AgilTrack from General Electric   http://venturebeat.com/2013/04/11/
                                    ge-agiltrac-hospital-hand-washing/

Sensor-crammed implant   http://www.extremetech.com/
                                    computing/151134-worlds-smallest-blood-
                                    monitoring-implant-talks-to-a-smartphone-
                                    but-whose

SRI International	http://www.sri.com
Nathan Collins	http://www.sri.com/newsroom/ press-releases/nathan-collins-joins-sri- international-executive-director-biosciences- divisi
BlueOregon	http://www.blueoregon.com/2009/09/ health-vs-health-care-a-false-choice/

Chapter 8

Wristbands	http://getpebble.com/
Footgear	http://www.caroltorgan. com/300-shoes-sensor-tech/
Rings	http://www.nngroup.com/articles/ javaring-wearable-computer/
Neckwear	https://plus.google.com/+Scobleizer/posts/ Mx1DHMdYKWn
Gordon Moore	http://en.wikipedia.org/wiki/Gordon_Moore
Moore's Law	http://www.webopedia.com/m/moores_law. html
Seymour Cray	http://en.wikipedia.org/wiki/Seymour_Cray
World's first supercomputer	http://www.thocp.net/hardware/cray_1.htm
Samsung Galaxy S4	http://dealnews.com/c672/Electronics/ Phones-Cell-Phones/Android-Phones/
Moore's law will vanish in about ten years	www.extremetech.com/compouting/165331- intels-former-chief-architect-moores-law- will-be-dead-within-a-decade
Nanotechnology	http://crnano.org/whatis.htm

Edward O. Thorp	http://en.wikipedia.org/wiki/ Edward_O._Thorp
Thorp wrote a book	http://www.amazon.com/Beat-Dealer-Winning-Strategy-Twenty-One/ dp/0394703103
Keith Taft	http://www.lolblackjack.com/blackjack/ professionals/keith-taft/
NagraID	http://www.nidsecurity.com/
AspenSnowMass	http://www.aspensnowmass.com/
One company is already working	http://bitly.com/11z6eFf
IMS Research estimate of wearables units	http://imsresearch.com/press-release/ Wearable_Technology_Market_to_Exceed_6_ Billion_by_2016d
Credit Suisse	http://blogs.barrons.com/ techtraderdaily/2013/05/17/aapl-goog-brcm-tops-in-credit-suisses-wearables-worldview/
Wearable technology called smart textiles	http://www.smart-textiles.net/stn/
Sensor-enabled clothing was introduced	http://edition.cnn.com/2013/07/25/tech/ innovation/bionic-fashion-wearable-tech-2015/index.html?hpt=hp_c5
Genevieve Dion	http://www.drexel.edu/westphal/contact/ directory/DionGenevieve/
Drexel University	http://www.drexel.edu/
Dion told the Christian Science Monitor	http://www.csmonitor.com/ Science/2013/0507/Wearable-computers-Marty-McFly-meet-your-jacket

Control it with your iPhone	http://www.latimes.com/news/science/ sciencenow/la-sci-sn-controlling- roboroach-cyborg-robot-cockroach -app-20130611,0,7847981.story
A bra that shocks assailants	http://www.wearable-technologies. com/2013/05/bras-with-superpowers/
First Warning Systems	http://www.firstwarningsystems.com/
A Stanford University team	http://inhabitat.com/stanfords-new-grid- scale-battery-can-last-for-1000-charge- cycles-without-degrading/
ABC news report on smart masks in Chinese cities	http://abcnews.go.com/International/chinas- filthy-air-prompts-mask-rush-cans-fresh/ story?id=18352787#.UZu1ICtas0A
Frog AirWaves	http://news.cnet.com/2300-17938_105- 10015813.html
iLocket from Dana	http://www.dano2.com/products/ iheart-locket
Brave New World	https://en.wikipedia.org/wiki/ Brave_New_World
1.7 million people have lost limbs	http://www.amputee-coalition.org/ fact_sheets/amp_stats_cause.html
Jesse Sullivan	http://vimeo.com/18477965
Dr. Todd Kuiken	http://www.ric.org/about/people/doctors/ detail/?id=78
Chris Tagatac	https://plus.google.com/+Scobleizer/ posts/1s6Z74Qr1gQ
Ekso Bionics	http://www.eksobionics.com/ekso

Bionic suits that enable paraplegics to walk	http://www.nytimes.com/2012/09/12/technology/wearable-robots-that-can-help-people-walk-again.html?_r=0
Physically handicapped people	http://www.ubergizmo.com/2012/09/toyota-creates-robots-to-help-disabled-persons/
Plantronics Voyager Legend	http://www.plantronics.com/us/product/voyager-legend?gclid=CJGZtvTIjLkCFcN_QgoddnwAIA
Joe Burton	http://www.plantronics.com/us/company/management/burton.jsp

Chapter 9

A complete reinvention of personal computing	http://en.wikipedia.org/wiki/Newton_(platform)
Google Now	http://www.google.com/landing/now/
First predictive search algorithm	http://www.wordstream.com/blog/ws/2013/06/24/predictive-search#.
EasilyDo	https://www.easilydo.com
Atooma	http://www.atooma.com/welcome
Gioia Pistola in June 2013, she said	https://plus.google.com/109177682016332485527
Spotify	https://www.spotify.com/us/
Tempo	http://scobleizer.com/2013/02/13/siris-contextual-sister-tempo-blows-away-apples-iphone-calendar
Dave Winer told this story	http://threads2.scripting.com/2013/june/aGoogleNowStory

Steve Brady, of Australia	https://plus.google.com/u/0/106586806505645886325/posts
Foreign Intelligence Surveillance Court (FISA)	http://en.wikipedia.org/wiki/United_States_Foreign_Intelligence_Surveillance_Court
Lola	http://www.sri.com/blog/meet-lola-virtual-personal-assistant-banking
Bill Mark	http://www.sri.com/about/people/william-mark
Dr. Michael Wolverton	http://www.ai.sri.com/people/mjw/

Chapter 10

Lockitron	https://lockitron.com/preorder
Z-wave	http://www.zwaveproducts.com/Zwave-Security/Zwave-Door-Locks.html
25 percent energy consumption reduction	http://www.spdcontrolsystems.com/
Smart glass industry	http://en.wikipedia.org/wiki/Smart_glass
A series of YouTube clips called *A Day Made of Glass*	http://www.youtube.com/watch?v=6Cf7IL_eZ38 and http://www.youtube.com/watch?annotation_id=annotation_424843&feature=iv&src_vid=6Cf7IL_eZ38&v=jZkHpNnXLB0
Entire surface is a touch-screen computer	http://www.dvice.com/archives/2012/01/samsung-now-sel.php
SmartThings	http://www.smartthings.com/
Alex Hawkinson	http://www.linkedin.com/in/ahawkinson

WigWag	http://www.wigwag.com/
Kickstarter	http://www.kickstarter.com/
CubeSensors	http://cubesensors.com
160 hours a month watching traditional TV	http://www.broadcastingcable.com/ article/493938-Nielsen_Time_Spent_ Watching_Traditional_TV_Up.php
NextGuide	https://plus.google.com/+Scobleizer/ posts/8uSVBNzZtSE
Vidora	http://www.vidora.com
Movea	http://www.movea.com/
Dave Rothenberg	http://www.linkedin.com/in/drothenberg
Orange, the French communications giant	http://en.wikipedia.org/wiki/ Orange_(telecommunications)
MoveaMobile	http://www.movea.com/applications/ mobile-devices
Leap Motion	https://www.leapmotion.com/
Power Glove	http://en.wikipedia.org/wiki/Power_Glove
Kinect measuring heartbeats	http://gizmodo.com/the-new-kinect- is-so-sensitive-it-can-read-your- heartbe-509073431
Blink	http://research.microsoft.com/en-us/um/ redmond/projects/blink/
MYO	https://www.thalmic.com/myo/
A YouTube video	http://www.youtube.com/ watch?v=oWu9TFJjHaM
Red Tomato Pizza	http://redtomato.biz/magnet/

Belkin	http://www.belkin.com
Philips	http://www.usa.philips.com/
Nest Thermostat	http://nest.com/blog/2013/07/18/ our-first-rush-hour-rewards-results/
PintoFeed	http://www.pintofeed.com/
Conserve Surge Protector	http://www.belkin.com/us/c/WSPWRCSR
Phantom power	http://electronics.howstuffworks.com/ everyday-tech/penny-pinching-save-energy-by.htm
Tom Raftery	http://es.linkedin.com/in/tomraftery
Greenmonk	http://greenmonk.net/author/tom/
WeMo	http://www.belkin.com/us/wemo
Outlets	http://www.belkin.com/us/wemo-switch
Motion sensors	http://www.belkin.com/us/ wemo-motion/p/P-F7C028-APL
Baby monitors	http://www.belkin.com/us/wemo-baby
Webcams	http://www.belkin.com/us/wemo-switch
Belkin's Echo	http://online.wsj.com/article/PR-CO-20130430-906312.html
Eco Sensor Water-Saving Tap	http://www.youtube.com/ watch?v=cy702Za7V80
Grid IQ	http://www.gedigitalenergy.com/demandopt/ catalog/GridIQ.htm

The Times of India   http://articles.timesofindia.indiatimes.
                                        com/2012-07-22/people/32788213_1_maid-
                                        clean-home-eureka-forbes

Assistant Robot   http://www.youtube.com/
                                        watch?v=G5Vd9k3-3LM

Chapter 11

Response rate of just 0.5 percent   http://smallbusiness.chron.com/average-rate-
                                        return-direct-mail-campaign-23974.html

10 million emails for only $500   http://www.inboxinteractive.com/2010/09/
                                        buying-or-renting-email-lists-things-to-
                                        consider/

Software bot for mass emails   http://best-mass-mailer.soft32download.com/

AdSense   http://adsense.google.com

Steven Levy   http://www.stevenlevy.com/index.php/about

Doc Searls   http://blogs.law.harvard.edu/doc/

Cluetrain Manifesto   http://www.amazon.com/The-Cluetrain-
                                        Manifesto-Anniversary-Edition/
                                        dp/0465024092/ref=pd_sim_b_1

The Intention Economy-When   http://www.amazon.com/The-Intention-
Customers Take Charge   Economy-Customers-Charge/
                                        dp/1422158527

Priceline.com   http://www.priceline.com/

CrowdSPRING   http://www.crowdspring.com/

The One-on-One Future   http://www.amazon.com/
                                        The-One-Future-Don-Peppers/
                                        dp/0385485662

Salesforce.com   http://www.salesforce.com/

Boston Phoenix   http://deal.thephoenix.com/boston

Facebook mobile ads   http://www.bloomberg.com/news/2013-
                                        08-02/facebook-closes-above-38-ipo-price-
                                        amid-mobile-ad-gains.html

Pebble smartwatch   http://getpebble.com/

Computerized socks   http://www.popsci.com/technology/
                                        article/2013-06/wearable-computer-socks-
                                        guaranteed-be-smelliest-computers-you-own

"Pay per gaze" system   http://nyti.ms/1820lTN

Tagwhat   http://www.tagwhat.com/

ThinkNear   http://www.thinknear.com/

Telenav   http://www.telenav.com/products/tn/

PARC   http://www.parc.com/

Several promising technologies   http://scobleizer.com/2013/08/03/the-parc-
                                        tour-of-2013-printed-circuits-better-
                                        batteries-contextual-systems-and-more/

Contextual intelligence   http://www.parc.com/news-release/80/parc-
                                        announces-contextual-intelligence-software-
                                        platform-for-automotive-industry.html

Phone sensors to determine your   http://www.informationweek.com/byte/
mood   personal-tech/smart-phones/contextual-
                                        intelligence-smart-phones-to/240009342

The Hidden Persuaders   http://en.wikipedia.org/wiki/Vance_Packard

Chapter 12

Bradley Manning	http://en.wikipedia.org/wiki/ Bradley_Manning
Dzhokhar and Tamerlan Tsarnaev	http://en.wikipedia.org/wiki/ Dzhokhar_and_Tamerlan_Tsarnaev
Edward Snowden	https://www.google.com/ search?q=snowden+interview
Google wrote an open letter	http://www.huffingtonpost.com/2013/06/11/ google-nsa-national-security_n_3423064. html
Google single privacy policy page	http://www.google.com/policies/privacy

Epilogue

Charity:water	http://www.charitywater.org/

Acknowledgements

Guy Kawasaki	http://www.guykawasaki.com/
Shawn Welch	http://amzn.to/Shawn-Welch
APE: Author, Publisher, Entrepreneur | How to Publish a Book	http://amzn.to/APEtheBook
Rick Smolan	http://www.amazon.com/Rick-Smolan/e/ B001ILM7W4
The Human Voice of Big Data	http://www.amazon.com/ Human-Face-Big-Data/dp/1454908270/

Harry Miller

http://www.linkedin.com/in/
harrymillerprofile/

Tema Goodwin

http://www.linkedin.com/pub/
tema-goodwin/3a/24b/9b

Rick Ladd

http://www.linkedin.com/in/rickladd

Nicholas DeLuca

http://www.linkedin.com/pub/
nicholas-deluca/12/14a/869

Shonali Burke

http://shonaliburke.com/

Acknowledgments

I t took a global village to write this book. We are great believers in crowd-sourcing, and in the 16 months we spent researching, writing, designing and producing *Age of Context*, more than a thousand people have helped us in ways large and small.

We are grateful to the dynamics of online conversations where people from more than a dozen countries commented, contributed, criticized, corrected and encouraged us through Facebook, Google+, Twitter and email. They were the sources of many new ideas and content that was included in this work. They corrected facts and focused observations.

Thank you, crowd. You helped us write a better book. As we enter a period where an increasing number of authors will self-publish, as we have done, the voluntary resources available to you are an asset not to be underestimated. Most authors just use social media as a promotional tool, and it is useful in that way; but it is far more powerful as a *conversational tool*, which is how we have used it.

Many individuals deserve mention as well. First, there are our mentors, professionals who have successfully blazed the trail we have followed.

Guy Kawasaki,[†††] and Shawn Welch[†††] of A*PE: Author, Publisher, Entrepreneur | How to Publish a Book*[†††] wrote the guidebook to how self-publishing should be done. Guy met with us and convinced us that this was the right course with us. Shawn did the internal design for *Age of Context*, shared both contacts and technical expertise that have proven invaluable.

Rick Smolan,[†††] who is co-author with Jennifer Erwitt of numerous popular and breathtaking photobooks, including *The Human Voice of Big Data.*[†††] Rick was the first to turn to the private sector to underwrite book projects without sacrificing editorial credibility.

Without the sponsorship of Rackspace, EasilyDo, Betaworks, Autodesk, Microsoft and Mindsmack, this book would not have been possible. Their generosity allowed Shel Israel to work full time on this project and to bring in a top-level team that has contributed far more than the authors had the right to expect:

- Harry Miller,[†††] former editor of PC World, added unbeliev-able insight and wisdom. He kept the authors on track and set a very high bar for accuracy and balance. He managed the editorial process and assembled a first-rate editorial team of Tema Goodwin[†††] our copy editor, Rick Ladd,[†††] proofreader and Nicholas DeLuca[†††] our fact checker.

- Shonali Burke[†††] has run our marketing and PR launch efforts, serving as the glue that holds together two authors who tend to simultaneously run out of control in divergent directions. She put together our incredibly successful launch party at the amazing Hiller Aviation Museum and managed our crammed speaking and media engagement schedule. She executed flawlessly, and exhibited intelligence, patience and integrity at every step.

- Nico Nicomedes, our cover designer, found us on Facebook, when we were floundering with several cover design attempts that the Facebook crowd, n its infinite wisdom had rejected. He was one of several people who voluntarily sent us rough cover designs, all of which were better than our selections. We liked Nico's because it was bold, memorable and reflected what we felt the book was about. He was fast and extremely easy to work with.
- Paula Israel conducted the "wife test," for this book as she has done for Shel's previous writings. Her job was to ensure that the language and content was interesting and useful to people outside of tech inner circles. In short, she made the book useful to more people

We thank all these people for their generosity. And finally, we thank each of you who have now read our book for your time, interest and support.

Index